Free Campers

• GUIDE TO NORWAY 2019 •

© 2018, 2019 ReiseMedia AS

ISBN 978-82-690997-0-6
Freecampers Guide to Norway
1. issue, 1.edition 2019

MAPS
Statens Kartverk, QGIS 3.0

DESIGN
Tor Nordahl, Aleksey Belyalov

PRINT
LaserTrykk.no

CONTACT
ReiseMedia AS
Fjuktjennveien 69
N-1930 Aurskog
Norway
tor@reisemedia.no

ISBN 978-82-690997-0-6

9 788269 099706 >

Foreword

This book is designed for campers in Norway. The book should make it easier to plan your trip and to be a useful aid and referencetool during your journey. The focus is on free campsites in the wild, but we will also include a selection of free parking near cities or other attractions. We have included an overview of service stations so You can stay totally independent of established campsites or camperstops if You want.

The author uses mostly free campsites in the beutiful Norwegian nature whenever possible or practical. It is often practical to alternate between established campsite / camperstops at uneven intervals on my journeys in Norway. I think it's ok to charge the batteries, drain the toilet, and fill the water quite often.

Norway is a unique country with a lot of beautiful nature. Everyone has the right to travel, camp and harvest from nature with certain limitations (Allemannsretten is described in a separate chapter). It is important to protect these rights by removing all traces of an overnight stay and leave the site in the same condition (or better) than when you arrived!

Nature is very vulnerable, and if «Allemannsretten» leads to excessive wear and tear on nature, you will soon see limitations in these freedoms. So -SHOW CAUTION- and remember the slogan:

NORWAY-POWERED BY NATURE.

Chapters

6

How to

How to use this guide 6
Symbols 8
GPS and QR-Readers 9

10

Right to roam

Right to roam (Allemannsretten) 10
Right to roam and the campervan 12
Overview 13

14

01 – South

Vest-Agder • Aust-Agder • Telemark

Freecamps 16
Parking 32
Rest Areas 36
Service Areas 40

44

02 – SouthEast

Vestfold • Østfold • Buskerud • Oslo • Akershus

Freecamps 46
Parking 60
Rest Areas 68
Service Areas 72

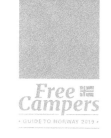

03 - NorthEast
Oppland • Hedmark

Freecamps...............78
Parking...............98
Rest Areas...............106
Service Areas...............112

04 - SouthWest
Rogaland • Hordaland • Sogn og Fjordane

Freecamps...............116
Parking...............128
Rest Areas...............136
Service Areas...............142

05 -Middle
Møre og Romsdal • Trøndelag

Freecamps...............148
Parking...............160
Rest Areas...............168
Service Areas...............172

06 -North
Nordland • Troms • Finnmark

Freecamps...............178
Parking...............194
Rest Areas...............202
Service Areas...............210

How to use this guide

The guide are organized in six sections for different parts of Norway. The sections are starting in the south and ending in the north. Each section are divided in parts for Freecamps, Free parkings, Rest Areas and Service Areas.

Section 1 — Southern part
Section 2 — SoutEastern part
Section 3 — NorthEastern part
Section 4 — SouthWestern part
Section 5 — NorthWestern part
Section 6 — Northern part.

For a detailed map of the location and borders for each section refer to the map on the first page of the section of interest.

A section starts with a map with indications for ALL sites of all types in this area of Norway. It also contains a short description of each county covered by the section. The parts for the different types of sites starts with a map for all sites of only this type.

Sites of different types are indicated with a symbol and a number for easy identification of which part and page to look for the detailed description of a site.

 Freecamp

 Free Parking

 Rest Area

 Service Area

Freecamps — Sites where you can camp for several nights and use camping-gear outside. These sites are indicated by small triangle and are always indicated by a green color throughout the book.

Free Parking — Sites where you can park for free. You can not stay for more than 24 hours and you should NOT use camping-gear outside. These sites are indicated by a blue circle and are always indicated by a blue color.

Rest Areas — Sites for resting by the roadside. It is FORBIDDEN to use camping-gear outside, but there are often tables and other facilities on the site. Do not stay for longer than 24 hours. These sites are indicated by a yellow square and are also indicated by a yellow color.

Service Areas — Sites for emptying Your toilet and graywater. Often possible to fill fresh-water. These sites are indicated by a red circle and are always indicated by a red color.

Number referring
to the map for
this section

Name of the site

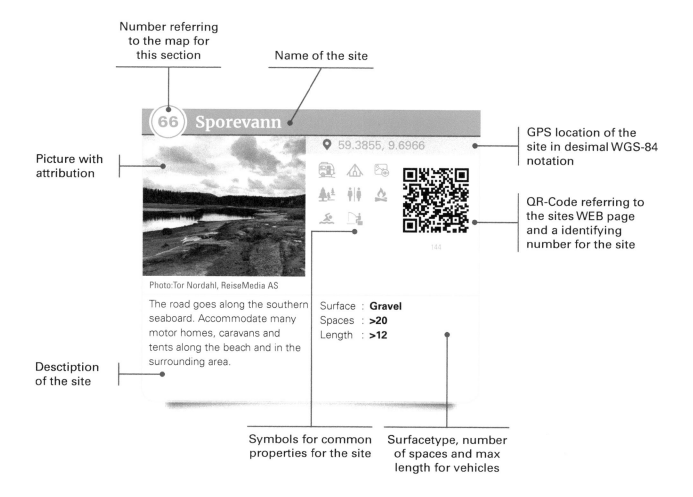

66 Sporevann

📍 59.3855, 9.6966

GPS location of the
site in desimal WGS-84
notation

Picture with
attribution

QR-Code referring to
the sites WEB page
and a identifying
number for the site

144

Photo:Tor Nordahl, ReiseMedia AS

The road goes along the southern
seaboard. Accommodate many
motor homes, caravans and
tents along the beach and in the
surrounding area.

Surface : **Gravel**
Spaces : **>20**
Length : **>12**

Desctiption
of the site

Symbols for common
properties for the site

Surfacetype, number
of spaces and max
length for vehicles

GREEN = Freecamp
BLUE = Free parking
ORANGE = Rest Area
RED = Service Area

Symbols

Open or accessible all year		Caravans OK
Tents allowed		Possibilities for bathing
Freshwater fishing		Saltwater fishing
Fire-pit/Grilling		Shelter
Picnic table		Trash disposal
Beautiful scenery		Near Point Of Interest
Forest Area		Mountain Area
Sea Area		Near/In Town
Toilets		Showers
Electricity		WiFi
Freshwater		Chem-toilet disposal
Wastewater disposal		Footpaths
Ski-trails		Slalom slopes

GPS and QR-Readers

All positions in this book are noted in desimal WGS-84 (World Geodetic System). This system are used by Global Positioning System (GPS) satelites that provides geolocation and time information to most positioning devices on the civilian matket. Most GPS devices will accept positioning input in desimal WGS-84 notation.

Read Your GPS user manual for futher information on how to input positions in desimal form.

The QR codes in this book encodes URL's to the different sites WEB page. From the WEB page You will be able to download the coordinates directly to your smartphone's map and start to navigate to the site. You will also find more pictures, 360 degree photos, videos and other information if available. On the WEB page You will be able to upload more pictures and give descriptions or feedback to the editor.

The camera app on iPhone are capable of reading QR codes but are somewhat limited in functionality. On Android phones You must download a reader from Google Play.

There are a lot of free QR-code readers for download to your smart devices. Personally I find TapMedia's QR Reader to be a good choice. QR Reader is a 100% free QR code scanner for the iPhone, Android, Windows Phone and Blackberry. It only works with QR codes, however it is fast and effective. When you open the app, it will open in real-time scanning mode ready to auto-detect a QR code. QR codes can be shared using Facebook, Twitter, Email and other social sharing sites. With it's integrated map view and integrated web browser, QR codes can be quickly scanned and viewed without ever leaving the app.

NeoReader is a cross-OS QR code reader that scans QR codes, DataMatrix, Aztec, EAN and UPC codes. It is simple to use with an elegant UI. NeoReader saves vCards and MECARDs directly to your phone contacts. Another great feature of NeoReader is the ability to view the history of previously scanned codes.

Right to roam (Allemannsretten)

OUTDOOR RECREATION IS AN IMPORTANT PART OF OUR CULTURAL HERITAGE IN NORWAY. SINCE ANCIENT TIMES, WE HAVE HAD THE RIGHT TO ROAM FREELY IN FORESTS AND OPEN COUNTRY, ALONG RIVERS, ON LAKES, AMONG THE SKERRIES, AND IN THE MOUNTAINS – IRRESPECTIVE OF WHO OWNS THE LAND.

We are allowed to harvest nature's bounty – which means not only saltwater fish, berries, mushrooms and wildflowers, but also our sensory impressions of the whole outdoor experience. The main principles of the right to roam are legally enshrined in the Outdoor Recreation Act of 1957. The right to roam applies to open countryside, where the following activities are permitted:

— Free movement on foot and on skis
— Resting and overnight camping
— Riding and cycling on trails and roads
— Swimming, canoing, rowing and sailing
— Picking berries, mushrooms and wildflowers
— Fishing without a license for saltwater species
— Hiking and Skiing

General Information on the Right to Roam

To fish in inland waters, you need a fishing permit from the landowner. If you are under 16, you can fish free of charge between January 1 and August 20, except where there are salmon, sea trout and sea char. To hunt, you need the permission of the landowner, who owns the hunting rights. You also need to pass the hunter accreditation exam and purchase a hunting license.

Do not enter cultivated or built-up land: fields, meadows, pastures, gardens, courtyards, building plots and industrial sites without permission. You do have access to some cultivated land, such as fields and meadows, between October 15 and April 30 when the ground is frozen or covered in snow. Please note that cultivated land need not actually be fenced off.

Always close gates and respect livestock, whether you are on cultivated or on uncultivated land. Dogs must be kept on a leash between April 1 and August 20. Be careful around fire – you must not light a fire in or near woodland between April 15 and September 15. Find out about any local bylaws regarding dog leashing and bonfires, which are often stricter than the national regulations. Make sure you tidy up before leaving your picnic spot or campsite. Take any litter away with you, leaving nothing behind.

Camping

In open country in the lowlands, you can pitch a tent and camp overnight for up to 48 hours in one location without prior permission from the landowner. In the mountains, and in remote, sparsely populated areas, you may camp for longer than 48 hours.

Unless local bylaws provide otherwise, you must never pitch your tent within 150 metres (500 feet) of an inhabited house or cabin. Always take care not to damage young trees. Remember, you must not camp on fenced land without the landowner's permission. You may light a fire in open country, but not in or near woodland between April 15 and September 15. Don't damage trees when gathering wood for your fire – use old, dry branches and twigs. If you build a bonfire on the shore, don't place it directly on rock, as this may cause the rock to split.

Fishing

You can fish with rod and line for saltwater species year-round, from a boat or from the shore. You may also fish in the sea free of charge for salmon, sea trout and sea char year-round, using

a rod from the shore, but local bylaws may include exceptions to this general rule. Sea fishing is not permitted within 100 metres (325 ft) of a river mouth during the conservation season. To fish for salmon, sea trout and sea char in rivers and lakes, you must purchase a fishing licence from the government and usually also a fishing permit from the landowner. If you are under 16, you can fish free of charge for inland species between January 1 and August 20, except where there are salmon, sea trout and sea char. Under-16s are not allowed to catch crayfish or to fish in man-made fish dams. Some lakes and rivers may be exempt from these rules, in which case signs should be displayed stating that free fishing does not apply. Before starting to fish, you must familiarize yourself with the fishing regulations.

Hiking and skiing
Hiking and skiing are freely permitted in open countryside in summer and winter alike. You can follow hiking trails, private roads and groomed ski trails or strike out on your own
In the winter you are also allowed to cross frozen or snow-covered fields and meadows. You may use paths and roads across fenced land year-round, so long as you keep your distance from farmyards, houses and cabins.

In open country, you can stop and rest where you wish, but please stay clear of inhabited houses and cabins, and be considerate of other visitors. You may light a fire in open country, but not in or near woodland between April 15 and September 15. Don't damage trees when gathering wood for your fire – use old, dry branches and twigs. If you build a bonfire on the shore, don't place it directly on rock, as this may cause the rock to split.

Picking berries, mushrooms and plants
Grab your basket or pail so you can pick berries, mushrooms, wildflowers and wild herb roots in open country and take them home with you.

Please note that special rules apply to picking cloudberries in the counties of Nordland, Troms and Finnmark, where landowners or users can prohibit picking. Any such prohibition must be notified through clear signposting, a newspaper announcement or equivalent means. Unless expressly prohibited in this way, cloudberries can be picked freely. In these counties owners can issue prohibitions in relation to cloudberry fields. These are areas of cloudberry plants, regardless of their location, which are so large and productive that they are of significant financial value to the landowner. Even if a cloudberry field is covered by a prohibition, you are still always allowed to pick cloudberries that you eat on the spot. On public land in Finnmark, everyone can pick cloudberries for personal consumption, but only Finnmark residents can pick them to sell. Be careful when collecting other natural products such as rocks, minerals, peat, moss and lichen. Ask the landowner's permission before taking any holly, burls, roots or bark.

More information : www.environmentagency.no

Right to roam and the campervan

WHERE CAN YOU DRIVE, WHERE KAN YOU STAY AND WHERE CAN YOU CAMP?

Norway is an oasis in Europe when it comes to the possibility of staying by car outside camp-sites and caravan parks. Many people prefer to spend the night in the nature because it's free because we want and because we can. The campgrounds are often expensive and crowded, and with little ones with load voices from morning to late in the evening. Tranquility and real na-ture-experiences are rarely found in such places.

Right to roam

One can not drive the campervan everywhere without taking consideration. It is not that you can drive anywhere You are able to access or where there are some wheel tracks. If you're in doubt if there's a road - it's NOT a road. You can drive on private roads as long as it is not blocked by a barrier or is signed that traffic is forbidden without permission from the landlord. Despite these obstacles there are still many public roads and toll roads that can be used to find accommoda-tion.

We often distinguish between "freecamping" and "wildcamping" where freecamping is consid-ered legal and wildcamping is illegal. You can stay along or in connection with a road = Free-camping. You can NOT drive into the terrain = Wildcamping.

In the lowlands the two-day rule applies. You can not stay longer than 2 days at the same site without the landowners permission. You can NOT camp less than 150 meters from a <u>inhabited</u> house or cottage.

Take care

If campervans and motorhomes are perceived as an increasing problem, new regulations are shure to come. If freecamping becomes an increasing pressure on nature with littering and wear, there will for shure be more and sharper regulations.

We therefore hope that you show consideration and leave the site in the same or better shape than you found it.

Remember : NORWAY POWERED BY NATURE

Overview

ALL SITES

Vest-Agder

The southernmost county in Norway, it includes the southernmost point of the entire country, Pysen island south of Mandal, and the southernmost part of continental Norway, Lindesnes. Population (2016) = 182.701 Most of the habitation lies along the coast, including the towns Kristiansand, Mandal, Flekkefjord and Farsund.

Aust-Agder

Located at the Skagerak coast and extends from Gjernestangen at Risør to the Kvåsefjorden in Lillesand. The inner parts of the county includes Setesdalsheiene and Austheiene. Population (2017) = 116.673 and about 78% of the inhabitants live in the costal municipalities of Arendal, Grimstad, Lillesand, Tvedestrand and Risør.

Telemark

The name means the "mark of the thelir", the ancient North Germanic tribe that inhabited this area. The county is located in southeastern Norway, extending from Hardangervidda to the Skagerak coastline. Telemark can be devided in four sub regions Kragerøregionen, Vest-Telemark, Øst-Telemark and Grenland. There are 8 towns in Telemark : Breivik, Kragerø, Langesund, Porsgrunn, Skien, Stathelle, Notodden and Rjukan. Population (2017) = 173.391

▲ — Free Camps

▲ — Parkings

▲ — Rest Areas

▲ — Service Areas

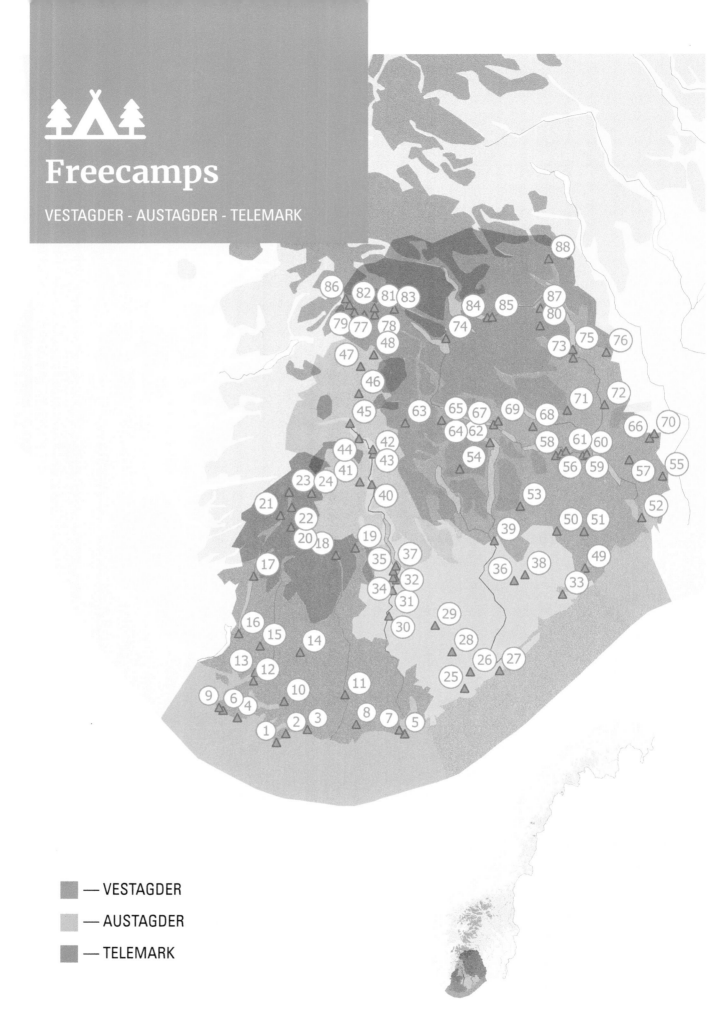

Freecamps

VESTAGDER - AUSTAGDER - TELEMARK

— VESTAGDER
— AUSTAGDER
— TELEMARK

1 Lindesnes fyr

📍 57.9851, 7.0486

Photo: Dimitriy Belyaev

Large gravel parking area often used by campers

Surface : **Asphalt**
Spaces : **>10**
Length : **>12**

2 Høylandskjæret

📍 58.0255, 7.1115

Photo: Maesel

Pier and emergency port facilities. Alternatively, you can park on GE Healthcare`s parking lot outside working hours. (58.0360, 7.1135)

Surface : **Gravel**
Spaces : **3**
Length : **<10**

3 Snig

📍 58.0528, 7.2710

Photo: Bjoertvedt

Here you can park at a large recreational area where there also is a sandy beach.

Surface : **Gravel**
Spaces : **5**
Length : **<10**

4 Haviksanden

📍 58.0678, 6.7289

Photo: Torstein Sunde

Parking for Listastrendene (beach). Long beautiful sandy beaches for swimming

Surface : **Gravel**
Spaces : **>15**
Length : **>12**

5 Flekkerøya

📍 58.0778, 8.0140

Photo: Sierra200

The pier at the marina. Also check out (58.0806, 7.9994) and parking lot at (58.0721, 7.9938)

Surface : **Asphalt**
Spaces : **10**
Length : **<12**

6 Nordhasselvika

📍 58.0906, 6.6139

Parking lot that can be used for free camping. Large recreational area with nice beaches, but the place is close to the road.

Surface : **Gravel**
Spaces : **5**
Length : **>10**

7 Møvik Fort

📍 58.0914, 7.9696

Quiet parking at the Møvik Fort, just a 10 minute drive from Kristiansand. Quiet and ideal spot for camping if you arrive from the ferry in the middle of the night.

Surface : **Gravel**
Spaces : **5**
Length : **<10**

8 Knuden

📍 58.0964, 7.6370

Photo: Bjoertvedt

Part of the old road with an old bridge. Possible to park a bit off the main road on the old road route for the smaller cars. Big cars can park at the picnic area. Worth seeing the bridge.

Surface : **Asphalt**
Spaces : **3**
Length : **<8**

9 Borshavn

📍 58.1000, 6.5811

Photo: Bjoertvedt

Gravel site at marina - free. Parking for motor homes with all amenities on (58.1006, 6.5826) NOK. 200, -

Surface : **Gravel**
Spaces : **5**
Length : **>12**

10 Møskeland

📍 58.1566, 7.0691

Large grass area with swimming possibility at the river Lyngna. Area can be closed out of season.

Surface : **Gras**
Spaces : **>10**
Length : **>10**

11 Marnardal

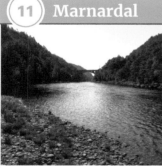

📍 58.2123, 7.5264

Photo: Allan Vendelbo

Gravel site along the road, toilet.

Surface : **Gravel**
Spaces : **2**
Length : **<10**

12 Handelandsvannet

📍 58.2258, 6.8172

Photo: Bjoertvedt

Small exit from the road, boat ramp. Near the road but a great view.

Surface : **Gras**
Spaces : **2**
Length : **<10**

13 Feda småbåthavn

📍 58.2620, 6.8211

255

Photo: Chell Hill

Lovely campsite with access to water, toilets and container for garbage.

Surface : **Asphalt**
Spaces : **>5**
Length : **>12**

14 Ulstjødn

📍 58.3661, 7.1456

1840

Photo: Aiwok

Parking for hiking in the area. Quiet road.

Surface : **Gravel**
Spaces : **<10**
Length : **>12**

15 Kongevollvatnet

📍 58.3724, 6.8342

92

Swimmingarea with good parking. Possibillities for beach volleyball. Garbage disposal at the Coop store.

Surface : **Gravel**
Spaces : **>10**
Length : **>12**

16 Bakke Bru

📍 58.4128, 6.6573

88

Photo: Jarle Vines

Swimming area with parking

Surface : **Gravel**
Spaces : **3**
Length : **>10**

17 Tonstad

📍 58.6596, 6.7160

1838

Photo: Sjaak Kempe

Parking at the marina

Surface : **Asphalt**
Spaces : **>5**
Length : **<12**

18 Ljosland skisenter

📍 58.7845, 7.3312

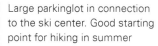

965

Photo: Mikkifs

Large parkinglot in connection to the ski center. Good starting point for hiking in summer

Surface : **Gravel**
Spaces : **>20**
Length : **>12**

19 Bortelid

📍 58.8230, 7.4748

Photo: Carsten R D

Large parking lot in connection to the alpine resort. Plenty of room in the summer.

Surface : **Asphalt**
Spaces : **>20**
Length : **>12**

20 Raudåvatnet

📍 58.8781, 6.9575

Photo: Ethaugen

Large parking lot for hikes in Setesdalsheiene

Surface : **Gravel**
Spaces : **>50**
Length : **>12**

21 Sinnes – Sirdal

📍 58.9200, 6.8639

Photo: Ronny B. Hagen

Large parking lot at the alpine resort. Also check Sinnesvatn (58.9152, 6.8664) for parking down by the water.

Surface : **Gravel**
Spaces : **>20**
Length : **>12**

22 Fidjeland – Sirdal

📍 58.9584, 6.9444

Photo: AkkuratD

Parking lot in connection to the alpine resort. Great site and few people in the summer. You can get elctricity and water from the hotel.

Surface : **Gravel**
Spaces : **>20**
Length : **>12**

23 Ådneram skitrekk

📍 59.0184, 6.9085

Photo: Racime

Parking at the ski lift - the ski lift is only open Friday-Saturday-Sunday during the season.
Great base for hiking in summer.
Several large parking lots in the area.

Surface : **Gravel**
Spaces : **>20**
Length : **<12**

24 Heiestøl

📍 59.0255, 7.0843

Take the side road down to the power station. Several sites along the road down to the water.
There are many nice free camp sites along Suleskarveien such as (59.0314, 7.0483) - (59.0319, 7.2644) - (59.0345, 7.1360) - (59.0445, 7.1689)

Surface : **Asphalt**
Spaces : **5**
Length : **>12**

25 Svennevig Bru

📍 58.2887, 8.4354

Public recreational area with nice swimming possibilities. Next to the road. Also check out great sites at (58.2893, 8.4377) and (58.2890, 8.4396)

Surface : **Gravel**
Spaces : **>10**
Length : **<12**

26 Lundesanden

📍 58.3600, 8.4661

Recreational area with large area for parking. Could be a lot of people in summer season. Toll road NOK. 20, -?

Surface : **Gravel**
Spaces : **>10**
Length : **<10**

27 Storesand

📍 58.3764, 8.6889

Photo: Tor Nordahl, ReiseMedia AS

Parking at recreational area and beautiful sandy beach.

Surface : **Gras**
Spaces : **>10**
Length : **>12**

28 Jernestangen

📍 58.4355, 8.3091

Large recreational area towards the water.

Surface : **Gravel**
Spaces : **>20**
Length : **>12**

29 Prestesundet

📍 58.5382, 8.1573

Photo: Bjoertvedt

Gravel site for camping. Great starting point for fishing.

Surface : **Gravel**
Spaces : **3**
Length : **<10**

30 Bjorå

📍 58.5574, 7.7935

Photo: Krg

Small freecamp between the road and a small lake.

Surface : **Gravel**
Spaces : **1**
Length : **<8**

31 Bygelandsfjord - Småbåthavna

📍 58.6658, 7.8014

Photo: OleKj

Free camping at the pier.

Surface : **Gravel**
Spaces : **>5**
Length : **10**

32 Grendi

📍 58.7109, 7.8222

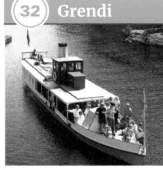

Photo: Odd Jarle Jørgensen

A small part of the old road that has been preserved. Lovely place .

Surface : **Gravel**
Spaces : **2**
Length : **<8**

33 Båssvika

📍 58.7165, 9.1192

Photo: Peulle

Small place by the sea. Near the road.

Surface : **Gravel**
Spaces : **3**
Length : **<10**

34 Prestnes

📍 58.7187, 7.7946

Photo: Toreid

Great secluded place! Excellent for tents.

Surface : **Gras**
Spaces : **3**
Length : **<10**

35 Daleviki - Byglandsfjord

📍 58.7458, 7.7890

Photo: clint3

Campground and recreational area overlooking Bygelandsfjorden.

Surface : **Gras**
Spaces : **>5**
Length : **<10**

36 Jåvnesmyra

📍 58.7550, 8.7338

Photo: zippo123

Free Camping/recreational area

Surface : **Gravel**
Spaces : **2**
Length : **<10**

37 Revviki – Byglandsfjorden

📍 58.7676, 7.8050

Photo: Huber Thilo

Here you can park undisturbed even though it is close to the road. Just off the old road.

Surface : **Gravel**
Spaces : **2**
Length : **>12**

38 Kvernvannet

📍 58.7835, 8.8134

Photo: Ola Haakon Berger

Large recreational area. Picnic tables, swimming possibilities.

Surface : **Gravel**
Spaces : **>10**
Length : **>12**

39 Sjodiplane

📍 58.9105, 8.5494

Photo: Tor Nordahl, ReiseMedia AS

Large recreational area with many secluded spots between Sjodiplane and Nidelva.

Surface : **Gravel**
Spaces : **>10**
Length : **>12**

40 Rysstad

📍 59.0891, 7.5463

Photo: Bjoertvedt

Beautiful spot by the river. Next to soccer field with lots of picnic tables and firepit. Might not be good if there are events happening at the stadium.

Surface : **Gravel**
Spaces : **5**
Length : **<10**

41 Brokke

📍 59.0945, 7.4510

Photo: Hesselhaker

Large gravel parkinglot at the alpine resort. Plenty of room in the summer but can be cramped during weekends and hollidays in the winter.

Surface : **Gravel**
Spaces : **>20**
Length : **>12**

42 Valle

📍 59.2151, 7.5320

Photo: Karl Ragnar Gjertsen

Small site down toward the river. Norway's best picnic area (Honnevje 59.2312, 7.5303) just nearby where there is room for several cars.

Surface : **Gravel**
Spaces : **2**
Length : **<8**

43 Dalsmo

⚷ 59.2330, 7.5231

Photo: Leo-setä

A good spot in the end of dirt road. Other possibilities at (59.2326, 7.5143) - (59.2306, 7.5053)

Surface : **Gras**
Spaces : **>5**
Length : **<8**

44 Holebekk

⚷ 59.2717, 7.4042

Photo: Bjoertvedt

Part of the old road with large recreational area down towards the river.

Surface : **Gravel**
Spaces : **>5**
Length : **<10**

45 Bykil

⚷ 59.3302, 7.3206

Photo: Geir Daasvatn

Part of the old road that bypasses the new tunnel. Space for accommodation along the way. Nice view.

Surface : **Gravel**
Spaces : **3**
Length : **<10**

46 Vatnedalsvatn

⚷ 59.4567, 7.3618

Photo: Philip Gabrielsen

Large parking at the dam. Nice view. More options in the area under the dam and at (59.4690, 7.3639)

Surface : **Gravel**
Spaces : **>10**
Length : **>12**

47 Hovden

⚷ 59.5688, 7.3507

Photo: Bjoertvedt

Large gravel parking in connection to the alpine resort. Can be cramped on weekends and hollidays during the winter, but is well suited to free camping in the summer.

Surface : **Gravel**
Spaces : **>50**
Length : **>12**

48 Breivatn

⚷ 59.6224, 7.4445

Photo: Erlend Bjørtvedt

Site behind the parking lot down towards the water.

Surface : **Gravel**
Spaces : **4**
Length : **<10**

49 Kjølebrønnskilen

📍 58.8319, 9.2751

272

Photo: Sjaak Kempe

Large site (gravelfilling) on to the sea. This site can hold many cars if there is just some organization.

Surface : **Gravel**
Spaces : **10**
Length : **>12**

50 Vølandtjerna

📍 58.9735, 9.0297

275

Photo: Fjorstut

Best suited for smaller cars. Several spots to park along the gravel road. Virtually no traffic. Also see (58.9896, 9.0275) - Toll NOK 40.-

Surface : **Gravel**
Spaces : **<5**
Length : **<8**

51 Merkebekk

📍 58.9813, 9.2427

277

Photo: Tor Nordahl, ReiseMedia AS

Closed down landing pier with space for mobile homes or caravans. Great views over the water.

Surface : **Gravel**
Spaces : **5**
Length : **>12**

52 Brevik

📍 59.0571, 9.6860

1791

Photo: Sjaak Kempe

Parking at recreational area. Many trails in the area and it is close to Brevik centrum.

Surface : **Gravel**
Spaces : **>10**
Length : **>12**

53 Gautefall

📍 59.0612, 8.7256

942

Photo: Jan-Tore Egge

Parking at the alpine resort. Several large parking lots in the area.

Surface : **Gravel**
Spaces : **>20**
Length : **>12**

54 Napetjønn

📍 59.1905, 8.2226

292

Photo: Hans O. Sorteberg

Exit from the road down to the water for launching of boat. Only room for 1 car/caravan.

Surface : **Gravel**
Spaces : **1**
Length : **<10**

55 Lakssjø

📍 59.2338, 9.8234

Photo: Arnstein Rønning

Recreational and swimming area with great views over the water. Also check (59.2352, 9.8262) and (59.2475, 9.7916)

Surface : **Gravel**
Spaces : **<5**
Length : **<10**

56 Høgsvatn

📍 59.2824, 8.9684

Photo:Tor Nordahl, ReiseMedia AS

Site at the outskirts of Høgsvatn. Old sand pit. Toll road, NOK. 40, -

Surface : **Gravel**
Spaces : **1**
Length : **< 10**

57 Slettevann

📍 59.2900, 9.5498

Photo: Frrahm

Swimming area with parking.

Surface : **Gravel**
Spaces :
Length :

58 Fristjønn

📍 59.2918, 9.009

Photo:Tor Nordahl, ReiseMedia AS

Very idyllic site at the forest pond. No phone coverage ...

Surface : **Gravel**
Spaces : **2**
Length : **<8**

59 Nomevatn

📍 59.2919, 9.1794

Photo: Tor Nordahl, ReiseMedia AS

Large parking at the recreational area. Can be cramped for space on nice sunny days during the swimming season. Alternative accommodation in the picnic area at (59.2901, 9.1658) or (59.2893, 9.1576)

Surface : **Gravel**
Spaces : **<10**
Length : **>12**

60 Vrangfoss

📍 59.2999, 9.2113

Photo:Tor Nordahl, ReiseMedia AS

Several sites in this area. Parking on both sides of the canal locks. Nice picnic area on the way down to the power plant. There is a small site at the very end of the road down by the water just past the power station. See (59.2961, 9.2207)

Surface : **Gravel**
Spaces : **5**
Length : **<10**

61 Hogga sluser

📍 59.3038, 9.0442

Photo: Tor Nordahl, ReiseMedia AS

Large gravel site in connection to the canal locks. The sightseeing attractions are the canal locks and the nationally listed road "Murane". Opportunities on the other side of the canal. See motorhome parking at (59.3012, 9.0431)

Surface	:	**Gravel**
Spaces	:	**>10**
Length	:	**<12**

62 Vrådal

📍 59.3106, 8.4394

Photo: Vrådal Panorama

Parking at the alpine resort. Few people here in the summer.

Surface	:	**Gravel**
Spaces	:	**>20**
Length	:	**>12**

63 Hallbjønnsekken

📍 59.3566, 7.7548

Photo: Siri Johannessen

Large gravel parking lot.

Surface	:	**Gravel**
Spaces	:	**>10**
Length	:	**>12**

64 Lisleå

📍 59.3830, 8.0398

Great site next to the river. 100 meters from theroad but it is quiet at night.

Surface	:	**Gras**
Spaces	:	**1**
Length	:	**<8**

65 Åmlivatn

📍 59.3832, 8.0396

Nice site at the end of Åmlivatn. Close to the road but quiet and peaceful at night.

Surface	:	**Gravel**
Spaces	:	**1**
Length	:	**<10**

66 Sporevann

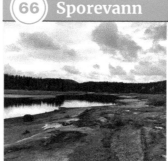

📍 59.3855, 9.6966

Photo:Tor Nordahl, ReiseMedia AS

The road goes along the southern seaboard. Accommodate many motor homes, caravans and tents along the beach and in the surrounding area.

Surface	:	**Gravel**
Spaces	:	**>20**
Length	:	**>12**

67 Sandodd

📍 59.3860, 8.4531

313

Photo: Morten Nærbøe

Site at the pier/marina.

Surface : **Gravel**
Spaces : **3**
Length : **<10**

68 Dalsvatn

📍 59.3940, 8.7655

196

Photo: Tor Nordahl, ReiseMedia AS

Recreational area down by the water with campground. Very little traffic on the gravel road that goes past.

Surface : **Gravel**
Spaces : **4**
Length : **<10**

69 Kviteseid

📍 59.4027, 8.4868

191

Photo:Erlend Bjørtvedt (CC-BY-SA)

Free campsite in city centre with a nice view of Kviteseidvatnet.

Surface : **Gravel**
Spaces : **>5**
Length : **>12**

70 Store Dalstjern

📍 59.4061, 9.7306

1809

Photo: Tor Nordahl, ReiseMedia AS

Idyllic place deep in the woods. A little close to the road, but very little traffic. Toll road.

Surface : **Gras**
Spaces : **2**
Length : **>10**

71 Lifjell

📍 59.4730, 9.0255

953

Gravel parking at the alpine resort. Several large parking lots in the area. Also try (59.4768, 9.0081)

Surface : **Gravel**
Spaces : **>10**
Length : **>12**

72 Hjuksevelta

📍 59.5092, 9.3174

326

Photo: Tor Nordahl, ReiseMedia AS

Beautiful recreational area with beach volleyball court, swimming, big lawns and a cozy little harbor.

Surface : **Gravel**
Spaces : **5**
Length : **<10**

73 Gransherad

📍 59.6900, 9.0344

Photo: Vidar Iversen

Lovely picnic area slightly secluded from the road. Great views across the river. More possibilities on both sides of the bridge.

Surface : **Gras**
Spaces : **>5**
Length : **>12**

74 Raulandsfjell

📍 59.7199, 8.0043

Photo: Stef James

Parking in connection to the alpine resort.

Surface : **Gravel**
Spaces : **>10**
Length : **>12**

75 Tinnoset

📍 59.7245, 9.0252

Photo: Jan-Tore Egge

Nice view of the water. Museum. Check also parking 59.7247, 9.0226

Surface : **Gravel**
Spaces : **>10**
Length : **<12**

76 Mjaugetjørn

📍 59.7254, 9.2960

Photo: Toktok

Several sites around the lake. See 59.7292, 9.2983 and 59.7301, 9.2988

Surface : **Gravel**
Spaces : **5**
Length : **<12**

77 Haukelifjell

📍 59.7799, 7.3329

Photo: Jacek Malczewski

Parking in connection to the alpine resort. There are several sites in the area that can be used for free camping.

Surface : **Gravel**
Spaces : **>20**
Length : **>12**

78 Kliningtjønn

📍 59.7850, 7.4158

Photo: alundy95

Right on to the water. Space enough for only one car/caravan at this site, but there are several opportunities along the road in this area. Fishing opportunities.

Surface : **Gravel**
Spaces : **>5**
Length : **<10**

79 Kjelavatn

📍 59.7862, 7.2522

Photo: TommyG

Several small sites along the road. Not suitable for the big or long cars...

Surface : **Gravel**
Spaces : **>5**
Length : **<8**

80 Vinsjehytta

📍 59.8093, 8.7470

Photo: Bjørn Strander

Area suitable for free camping. You may park at the parking lot at Vinsjehytta (cabin) or on the roads in the terrain on the other side. The weather here can change quickly.

Surface : **Gravel**
Spaces : **5**
Length : **>12**

81 Vågsli

📍 59.8137, 7.4068

Photo: O.Nestveit

Large recreational area by dam.

Surface : **Gras**
Spaces : **>10**
Length : **<10**

82 Ståvassdammen

📍 59.8138, 7.2053

Photo: Arnesten

Starting point for mountain hikes. Hiking trails go right past. More opportunities for free camping in the area.

Surface : **Gravel**
Spaces : **>5**
Length : **<10**

83 Songadammen

📍 59.8171, 7.5664

Photo: Geir83

Large site (grass) below the dam. Great hiking area.

Surface : **Gras**
Spaces : **>10**
Length : **<10**

84 Møsvatn

📍 59.8216, 8.3183

Photo: Jan-Tore Egge

Great view of Lake Møsvatn. Also check motorhome parking at 59.8168, 8.3117

Surface : **Gravel**
Spaces : **>10**
Length : **>12**

85 Frøystaul

⚲ 59.8259, 8.3558

1799

Photo: Jan-Tore Egge

Cabin area with several large sites for free camping. See also (59.8255, 8.3466) and (59.8258, 8.3455)

Surface : **Gravel**
Spaces : **>10**
Length : **>12**

86 Gautesvik

⚲ 59.8377, 7.1685

796

Photo: trolvag

In front of the lake, nice view. Toilet. Secluded spot for camper below the parking area

Surface : **Gravel**
Spaces : **>10**
Length : **>12**

87 Gaustablikk

⚲ 59.8810, 8.7369

941

Photo: G. Lanting

Parking in connection to the alpine resort.

Surface : **Gravel**
Spaces : **>20**
Length : **>12**

88 Hovmannsberget

⚲ 60.0865, 8.7640

120

Photo: Jan-Tore Egge

Recreational area down towards the river Austbygdåe.

Surface : **Gravel**
Spaces : **4**
Length : **<12**

31 •

Parking

VESTAGDER - AUSTAGDER - TELEMARK

■ — VESTAGDER

■ — AUSTAGDER

■ — TELEMARK

1 Tjusdalsbukta

📍 57.9905, 7.5302

Foto: Otto Reuber

Parking lot

Surface : **Asphalt**
Spaces : **>5**
Length :

2 Piren – Sjøsanden

📍 58.0210, 7.4554

Photo: Yosh3000

Parking close to Sjøsanden holi-
day complex. Great for spending
the night in the car but, use Sjøsanden camping (58.0197, 7.4396)
if you deside to stay in Mandal awhile.

Surface : **Asphalt**
Spaces : **>10**
Length : **<8**

3 Terneholmen

📍 58.0412, 7.1538

Photo: Ben Bender

Several possibilities in the area.
Restaurant "Under" opens here
in 2019. The restaurant will be
located 6 meters below sea
level. Also check out (58.0407, 7.1514) - (58.0398, 7.1501) - (58.0386, 7.1527)

Surface : **Asphalt**
Spaces : **>10**
Length : **<12**

4 Langviga

📍 58.0744, 7.8838

Photo: kalev kevad

Parking at swimming area.

Surface : **Gravel**
Spaces : **5**
Length : **<10**

5 Lista Fyr

📍 58.1093, 6.56910

Photo: Rolf Steinar

Paved parking for many cars. You
may rent rooms for the night.
Café and Gallery.

Surface : **Asphalt**
Spaces : **>20**
Length : **>12**

6 Kristiansand

📍 58.1435, 7.9822

Photo: Trolvag

Parking lot with free parking at
night and on Sundays. Also see
parking at (58.1451, 7.9835) -
(058.1430, 7.9922) - (58.1448,
8.0119)

Surface : **Asphalt**
Spaces : **>10**
Length : **<8**

7 Sørlandsparken

📍 58.1758, 8.1415

251

Large spacious sites at the shopping center carpark. GPS co-ordinates for quieter sites in the outskirts of the center. Emptying and refilling at Kristiansand Caravan AS (58.1729, 8.1327)

Surface : **Asphalt**
Spaces : **>50**
Length : **>12**

8 Dyreparken

📍 58.1808, 8.1490

1851

Great parking for visitors to the zoo.

Surface : **Asphalt**
Spaces : **>100**
Length : **>12**

9 Sørlandet Caravancenter

📍 58.3438, 8.5675

2

Parking outside the caravan center

Surface : **Asphalt**
Spaces : **>10**
Length : **>12**

10 Tingvatn

📍 58.3941, 7.2302

263

Large paved parking in connection with landmarks.

Surface : **Asphalt**
Spaces : **>20**
Length : **>12**

11 Sinnesvatn

📍 58.9152, 6.8669

1880

Photo: Carlos A Machado

Large gravel parking down by Sinnesvatn.

Surface : **Gravel**
Spaces : **>20**
Length : **>12**

12 Birtedalsvegen

📍 59.0796, 8.0313

285

Gravel parking lot.

Surface : **Gravel**
Spaces :
Length :

13 Kviteseid

📍 59.4027, 8.4868

315

Photo: trolvag

Large free parking in Kviteseid.

Surface : **Gravel**
Spaces : **5**
Length : **<12**

14 Stavsro

📍 59.8350, 8.7152

361

Photo: Bjoertvedt

Large parking lot with the possibility of accommodation. Recreational facilities and starting point for hikes to Gaustatoppen. Often full during the daytime. But new motorhome parking and expansion of parking lots are planned finished in 2019.

Surface : **Asphalt**
Spaces : **>20**
Length : **<10**

15 Rjukan

📍 59.8774, 8.5861

364

Photo: G.Lanting

Free parking spaces for campers. 6 places with free electricity.

Surface : **Gravel**
Spaces : **12**
Length : **<10**

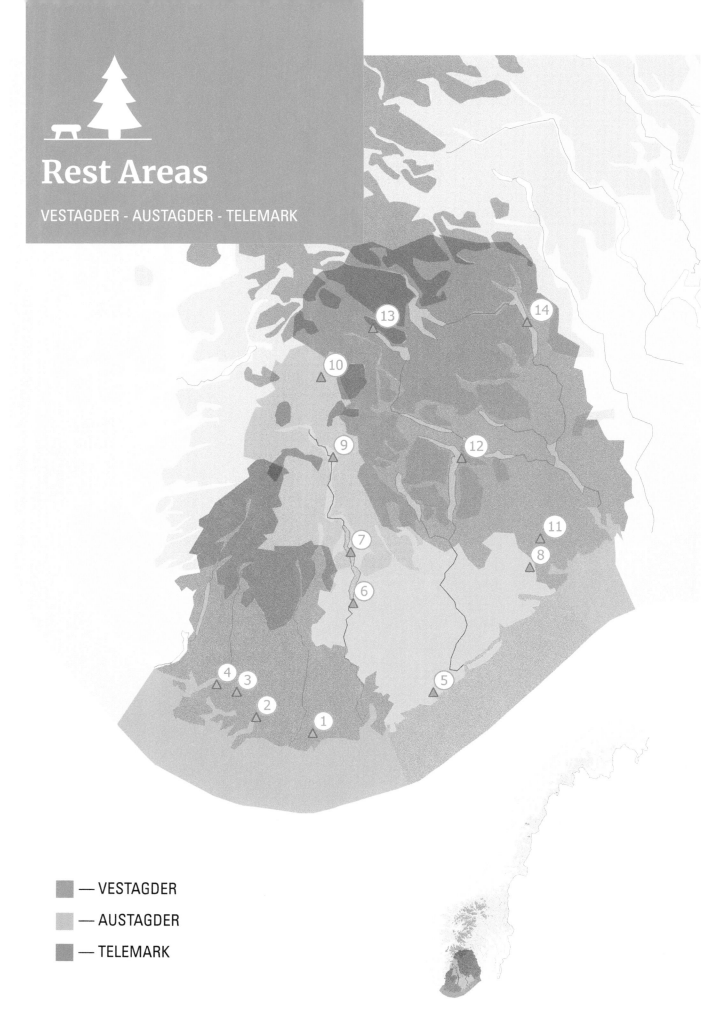

Rest Areas

VESTAGDER - AUSTAGDER - TELEMARK

— VESTAGDER
— AUSTAGDER
— TELEMARK

1 Suvatnet

📍 58.0868, 7.6211

247

picnic area

Surface : **Asphalt**
Spaces : **>5**
Length : **>12**

2 Lyngdal sør

📍 58.1261, 7.1838

248

picnic area

Surface : **Asphalt**
Spaces : **5**
Length : **>12**

3 Lyngdal nord

📍 58.2203, 7.0145

252

Picnic area with cafe

Surface : **Asphalt**
Spaces : **>10**
Length : **>12**

4 Teistedal rasteplass

📍 58.2417, 6.8545

254

Picnic area with facilities.

Surface : **Asphalt**
Spaces : **5**
Length : **>12**

5 Trolldalen

📍 58.3069, 8.4940

258

Large picnic area with facilities.
Trails and lookout tower on the
site. Free Wi-Fi.

Surface : **Asphalt**
Spaces : **>20**
Length : **>12**

6 Holteøyane rasteplass

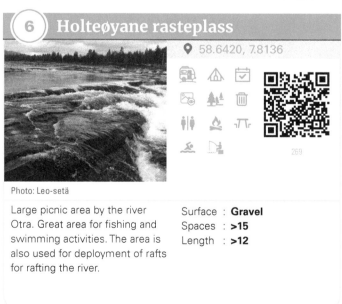

📍 58.6420, 7.8136

269

Photo: Leo-setä

Large picnic area by the river
Otra. Great area for fishing and
swimming activities. The area is
also used for deployment of rafts
for rafting the river.

Surface : **Gravel**
Spaces : **>15**
Length : **>12**

(7) Storstraumen

📍 58.8502, 7.7497

1817

Photo: Jan-Tore Egge

Parking and picnic area by the locks.

Surface : **Gravel**
Spaces : **>5**
Length : **>12**

(8) Østerholtsheia

📍 58.8598, 9.1359

1831

Large picnic area near the cozy water on both sides of E18. Withdrawn from the road.

Surface : **Asphalt**
Spaces : **>20**
Length : **>12**

(9) Honnevje

📍 59.2312, 7.5303

293

Photo: Randi Hausken

Swimming and picnic area, named Norway's finest in 2011.

Surface : **Asphalt**
Spaces : **>10**
Length : **>12**

(10) Hegni/Hovden

📍 59.5521, 7.3647

1834

Photo: G. Lanting

Parking at recreation area. Swimming, museum and canoe rentals.

Surface : **Asphalt**
Spaces : **>10**
Length : **>12**

(11) Båtødden

📍 58.9805, 9.1964

1873

Photo: Tor Nordahl, ReiseMedia AS

Exit from the road. Not suitable as a picnic area but you may park here for over night.

Surface : **Gravel**
Spaces : **>10**
Length : **>12**

(12) Sandbekk rasteplass

📍 59.2814, 8.5272

300

Photo: Aconcagua

Just off the waterfront.

Surface : **Asphalt**
Spaces : **>5**
Length : **>12**

13 Arabygdi

📍 59.7749, 7.7266

Photo: Jan-Tore Egge

346

Picnic area overlooking Totak. You will find the Statue of Myllarguten and some information at this site.

Surface : **Gravel**
Spaces : **>5**
Length : **>12**

14 Gravtjønn

📍 59.8613, 8.9377

Photo: Bengt Larsson

363

Picnic area, war memorial and information. Funny old locomotive. Views across Tinnsjøen.

Surface : **Asphalt**
Spaces : **>10**
Length : **>12**

Service Areas

VESTAGDER - AUSTAGDER - TELEMARK

— VESTAGDER

— AUSTAGDER

— TELEMARK

1 Mandal
📍 58.0203, 7.46305

Grønsvika wastewater treatment plant

2 Sprangereid
📍 58.0452, 7.14080

Spangereid Gasoline and Trade in Spangereid center on the way out towards Lindesnes Lighthouse

3 Kristiansand – Fidjane
📍 58.1452, 7.9118

Shell Fidje, both directions

4 Kristiansand – Sørlandsparken
📍 58.1725, 8.13255

Kristiansand Caravan, Sørlandsparken

5 Flekkefjord
📍 58.2927, 6.66303

Downtown Flekkefjord by the motorhome parking.

6 Lillesand – Langbrygga
📍 58.2469, 8.3785

Langbrygga

7 Lillesand – Kokkenes
📍 58.2474, 8.3837

Kokkenes motorhome parking

8 Grimstad – Caravansenter
📍 58.3391, 8.5671

Sørlandets caravan center

9 Grimstad – Circle K
📍 58.3419, 8.5685

Circle K Grimstad, Vesterled 100

10 Arendal
📍 58.4742, 8.7458

Circle K Harebakken

11 Hornnes
📍 58.5506, 7.7758

Parking for motorhomes at Setesdal Mineral Park at Hornnes

12 Risør – Circle K
📍 58.7174, 9.21321

Circle K Risør, Kragsgt. 140

13 Risør – Akvariet
📍 58.7182, 9.24009

By the aquarium, Strandgata 14 outermost in Strandgata

14 Åmli
📍 58.7645, 8.48237

Åmli packing station

15 Fiane
📍 58.8217, 9.0743

Cirkle K Brokelandsheia

16 Skarsmo
📍 59.4086, 7.4099

Picnic area - Only emptying chemical toilet - Closed during the winter.

17 Langesund
📍 59.0129, 9.74301

Parking for motorhomes by Skjærgårdshallen

1166

18 Stathelle
📍 59.0375, 9.67489

Shell Europaveien 139

1165

19 Drangedal
📍 59.0904, 9.06444

Circle K, Kåsmyra

1168

20 Telemarksporten
📍 59.1219, 9.70766

Circle K, Prestmoen 4

1171

21 Kjørbekkhøgda
📍 59.1774, 9.62570

Esso, Porsgrunnsvegen 125

1173

22 Ulefoss
📍 59.2821, 9.27132

Esso, Jernværksvegen 1

1169

23 Bø
📍 59.4127, 9.06886

Esso, Bøgata 79

1167

24 Seljord
📍 59.4841, 8.62832

Circle K, Brøløsvegen

1172

25 Notodden
📍 59.5595, 9.24849

By Nesøya motorhome parking - waste disposal units, also with shower and toilet

1170

26 Åmot
📍 59.5725, 7.99248

Free public waste disposal unit at Groven camping

1176

27 Krossen
📍 59.6970, 8.06489

Approximately 200 meters past Spar,by the garbage containers

1177

28 Svadde
📍 59.8796, 8.66110

Svadde industrial area, entry from RV37 by Dal church

1174

29 Austbygde
📍 59.9889, 8.81674

At Sandviken Camping

1175

VESTAGDER - AUSTAGDER - TELEMARK

Vestfold

Vestfold is a county in southern Norway, located on the west side of the Oslofjord and its arm Drammensfjorden. Extends westwards to the Langesund Fjord and the hills west of Lågendalen. The county includes the southernmost part of Lake Eikeren in the northwest. The largest cities are Tønsberg, Sandefjord, Larvik, Horten, Holmestrand and Stavern. Population (2017) = 249.063

Østfold

Østfold is the southeasternmost county. It lies between the Oslofjord in the west and the national border to Sweden in the east. To the north lies Akershus, and in the south Iddefjorden forms the border with Sweden. The largest cities are Fredrikstad, Sarpsborg, Moss, Halden, Askim and Mysen. Population (2017) = 295.421

Buskerud

Buskerud, county extending from Hurumlandet by the Oslofjord in the southeast to Hardangervidda and Hemsedalsfjella in the northwest. Buskerud includes the great valleys of Hallingdal and Numedal with forest and mountain tracts, including the eastern part of Hardangervidda in the west and Skarvheimen in the northwest. The largest cities are Drammen, Kongsberg and Hønefoss. Population (2017) = 281.769

Oslo

Oslo is Norway's capital and largest city, and one of the oldest towns in the country. Oslo also forms a municipality and an county and lies in the inner part of the Oslo Fjord, with the city center in the middle of the two cove Pipervika and Bjørvika. Population (2017) = 975.744

Akershus

Akershus is an county located around the inner Oslofjord and encloses Oslo, with the exception of the forest stretches in Nordmarka, where Oslo has a common border with Buskerud and Oppland. Largest cities are Ski, Jessheim and Drøbak. Population (2017) = 614.026

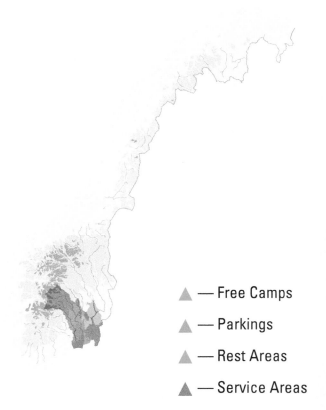

▲ — Free Camps

▲ — Parkings

▲ — Rest Areas

▲ — Service Areas

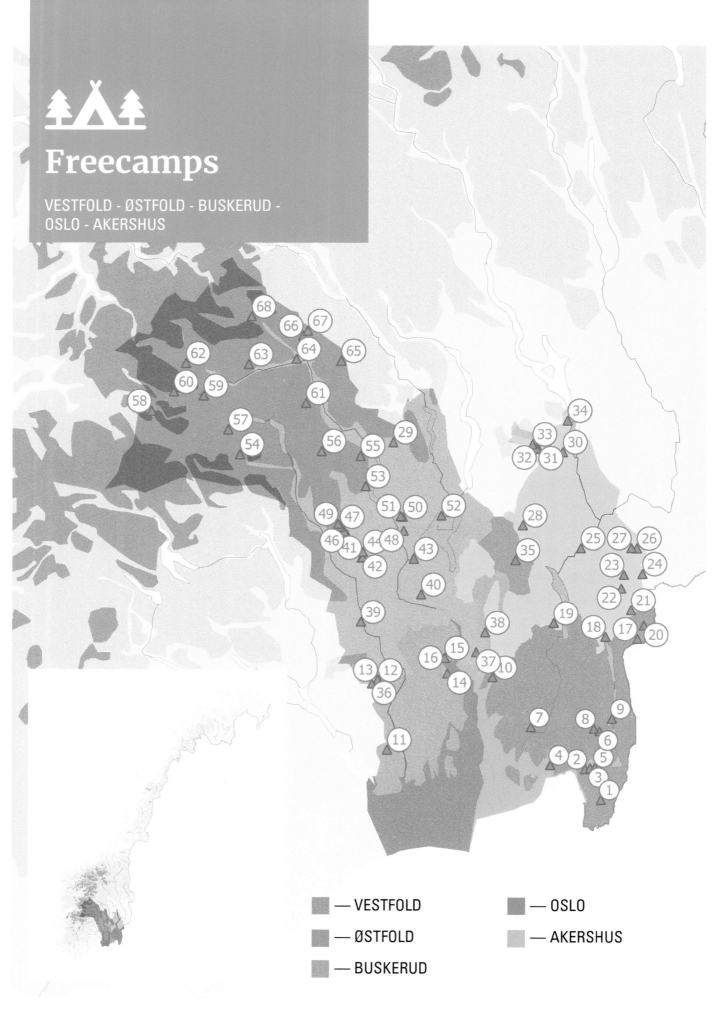

Freecamps

VESTFOLD - ØSTFOLD - BUSKERUD -
OSLO - AKERSHUS

— VESTFOLD
— ØSTFOLD
— BUSKERUD
— OSLO
— AKERSHUS

1 Bråtenetjern

📍 59.0039, 11.5864

Photo: Tor Nordahl, ReiseMedia AS

Great place in the forest. Hiking routes in the area and many pristine fishing waters inland. An abandoned farm nearby at 59.0013, 11.5776

Surface : **Gravel**
Spaces : **2**
Length : **<8**

2 Tistedalen Brygge

📍 59.1252, 11.4505

Photo: Tor Nordahl, ReiseMedia AS

Large gravel site at the pier. The Veteran ship MS Brekke has base at the pier. Departures on Wednesday, Friday and Sunday in the season which is from late June to late August.

Surface : **Gravel**
Spaces : **>10**
Length : **>12**

3 Vanninga

📍 59.1306, 11.4888

Photo: Tor Nordahl, ReiseMedia AS

Large recreational and swimming area at Femsjøen. Great views and a few facilities on site.

Surface : **Gravel**
Spaces : **>10**
Length : **>12**

4 Dusebukta

📍 59.1338, 11.1792

Photo: Softfocus

Parking at the swimming area and conservation area. Protected for biodiversity.

Surface : **Gravel**
Spaces : **5**
Length : **<10**

5 Kruseter

📍 59.1352, 11.5262

Photo: Tor Nordahl, ReiseMedia AS

Nice but small site right by the road. Great place to use in conjunction with a visit to the Brekke locks. More possibilities in the area both at rest areas and other parking facilities. Check 59.1338, 11.5308 to 59.1353, 11.5244 and 59.1351, 11.5163

Surface : **Gravel**
Spaces : **>10**
Length : **>12**

6 Søndre Hivann

📍 59.2814, 11.5449

Photo: Tor Nordahl, ReiseMedia AS

Several sites in the area (59.2814, 11.5426 and 59.2765, 11.5316). Landscaped recreational area with benches and toilet. The site at 59.2765, 11.5316 is suitable for tents. Toll road NOK. 50, -

Surface : **Gras**
Spaces : **5**
Length : **<12**

7 Soli badeplass

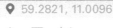

📍 59.2821, 11.0096

1659

Photo: Fredrikstad Kommune

Quite close to the road. Recreational area with swimming opportunities. The Viking ship "Tune ship" was found here. You can see the ship in Vikingskiphuset on Bygdøy in Oslo.

Surface : **Gravel**
Spaces : **3**
Length : **<10**

8 Djupetjernet

📍 59.2906, 11.5003

1872

Photo: Tor Nordahl, ReiseMedia AS

Great site for 1 car. Toll road NOK 50, -

Surface : **Gravel**
Spaces : **1**
Length : **<8**

9 Sambølsaga

📍 59.3351, 11.6383

1652

Photo: Tor Nordahl, ReiseMeida AS

Old abandoned sawmill and recreational area. Idyllic on warm summer evenings.

Surface : **Gravel**
Spaces : **5**
Length : **>10**

10 Kambo

📍 59.4765, 10.6865

1669

Photo: Tor Nordahl, ReiseMedia AS

Parking at the marina. Great place for fishing. Enormous free commuter parking lot at (59.4790, 10.6918) if there is no vacant parking at the marina.

Surface : **Gravel**
Spaces : **>5**
Length : **<10**

11 Roppestad

📍 59.1521, 9.9081

290

Large recreational area with free accommodation. Naturist beach on the northern part. Free camping for up to two days at a time.

Surface : **Gravel**
Spaces : **18**
Length : **>12**

12 Siljuvann

📍 59.4322, 9.7948

320

Photo: Tor Nordahl, ReiseMedia AS

Idyllic sites along the water. Also check out (59.4321, 9.7936)

Surface : **Gravel**
Spaces : **3**
Length : **>12**

13 Presteseter

📍 59.4342, 9.7905

Photo: Tor Nordahl, ReiseMedia AS

Great campsite overlooking the pond. Brilliant for tents with large grass area.

Surface : **Gras**
Spaces : **4**
Length : **>12**

14 Hagemannsparken

📍 59.4804, 10.3301

Photo: Tor Nordahl, ReiseMedia AS

Hagemann in Holmestrand is a part of a recreational area. The marina gives you access to a great green area where you can use the barbecue on site. Good fishing conditions.

Surface : **Gravel**
Spaces : **4**
Length : **<12**

15 Bekkestranda

📍 59.5431, 10.3009

Photo: Jan-Tore Egge

Relatively flat and large gravel site in which to park alongside to the seashore, 50m to the sandy beach, good fishing and sun conditions. Check out parking at (59.5520, 10.2859).

Surface : **Gravel**
Spaces : **10**
Length : **>12**

16 Brekkestranda

📍 59.5435, 10.3002

Gravel site with parking right down by the water. Fishing and swimming.

Surface : **Gravel**
Spaces : **>5**
Length : **>12**

17 Rømsjøen Syd

📍 59.6659, 11.8040

Photo: Tor Nordahl, ReiseMedia AS

Exit from the road (gravel). Fishing.

Surface : **Gravel**
Spaces : **5**
Length : **>12**

18 Skulerudsjøen

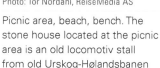

📍 59.6684, 11.5523

Photo: Tor Nordahl, ReiseMedia AS

Picnic area, beach, bench. The stone house located at the picnic area is an old locomotiv stall from old Urskog-Hølandsbanen (Tertitten). There is room for accommodation also there. (59.6704, 11.5474) shower facility at the marina.

Surface : **Gravel**
Spaces : **5**
Length : **<10**

19 Bermerud Badeplass

📍 59.7134, 11.1384

156

Photo: Tor Nordahl, ReiseMedia AS

Large parking at the swimming area in Lyseren.

Surface : **Gravel**
Spaces : **>10**
Length : **>12**

20 Sandvikssand

📍 59.7215, 11.8483

340

Photo: Tor Nordahl, ReiseMedia AS

Swimming and recreational area. No Camping on the beach, but you may use the space next to the recreational area for accommodation.

Surface : **Gras**
Spaces : **3**
Length : **<10**

21 Hallangen

📍 59.7838, 11.7417

347

Photo: Tor Nordahl, ReiseMedia AS

Lots of nice sites in the area. Also check out (59.7861, 11.7524) and (59.7870, 11.7536).

Surface : **Gravel**
Spaces : **>15**
Length : **>12**

22 Søndre Holtjenn

📍 59.8704, 11.6564

1929

Photo: Tor Nordahl, ReiseMedia AS

Small site at fishing spot. Near the road but almost no traffic at night.

Surface : **Gravel**
Spaces : **1-2**
Length : **<8**

23 Settetjenn

📍 59.9271, 11.6717

1927

Photo: Tor Nordahl, ReiseMedia AS

Large gravel site down by the lakeside. Great starting point for hikes in Mangenfjellet.

Surface : **Gravel**
Spaces : **<5**
Length : **>12**

24 Øysjøen

📍 59.9342, 11.8169

205

Photo: Tor Nordahl, ReiseMedia AS

Small site between the road and the water. Quiet road.

Surface : **Gravel**
Spaces : **2**
Length : **<10**

25 Rånåsfoss

📍 60.0262, 11.3166

Photo: Tor Nordahl, ReiseMedia AS

Recreational area near the power plant at Rånåsfoss

Surface : **Gravel**
Spaces : **5**
Length : **>10**

26 Rabbillen

📍 60.0370, 11.7627

Photo:Tor Nordahl, ReiseMedia AS

Very nice site suitable for accommodation. Fire place and toilet. Drive via 60.0261, 11.7653. Toll road NOK. 40, - http://news.reisemedia.no/2017/11/28/rabbillen/

Surface : **Gravel**
Spaces : **4**
Length : **>12**

27 Handsjøen

📍 60.0374, 11.7187

Photo:Tor Nordahl, ReiseMedia AS

Nice place at the small fishing lake, sheltered from the quite road.

Surface : **Gravel**
Spaces : **1**
Length : **<12**

28 Varingskollen

📍 60.1056, 10.8434

Photo: Tor Nordahl, ReiseMedia AS

Gravel parking (60.1056, 10.8434), asphalt parking (60.1060, 10.8456) and grass parking (60.1065, 10.8464) in connection to the alpine resort.

Surface : **Gravel**
Spaces : **>20**
Length : **>12**

29 Buvatnet

📍 60.4046, 9.7586

Photo: Tommy Gildseth

Several nice little sites along the water

Surface : **Gravel**
Spaces : **>5**
Length : **<10**

30 Minneåsen

📍 60.4121, 11.1274

Photo: Tor Nordahl, ReiseMedia AS

Several possibilities in the area of (60.4129, 11.1214) and secluded parking at (60.4115, 11.1206).

Surface : **Gravel**
Spaces : **>5**
Length : **>12**

31 Skrukkelisjøen

📍 60.4197, 10.9304

Photo: Tor Nordahl, ReiseMedia AS

Picnic area with great views. Fishing. Also check 60.4213, 10.9122 and several other opportunities along the water.

Surface : **Gravel**
Spaces : **3**
Length : **>12**

32 Skrukkelisjøen Midt

📍 60.4215, 10.9123

Photo: Tor Nordahl, ReiseMedia AS

Large gravel site facing the water.

Surface : **Gravel**
Spaces : **5**
Length : **>12**

33 Skrukkelisjøen Nord

📍 60.4365, 10.8789

Photo: Tor Nordahl, ReiseMedia AS

Two large open sites down towards Skrukkelisjøen. Also check (60.4372, 10.8774) nearby.

Surface : **Gras**
Spaces : **>10**
Length : **>12**

34 Atthaldsdammen

📍 60.5406, 11.1499

Photo:Tor Nordahl, ReiseMedia AS

Great starting point for hikes. Historical "Feiring Jerverk" is not far from here. Toll road NOK. 50, -

Surface : **Gravel**
Spaces : **4**
Length : **< 10**

35 Oslo skisenter – Trollvann

📍 59.9621, 10.8041

Photo: Tor Nordahl, ReiseMedia AS

Gravel parking in connection to the recreational area. Also see parking at (59.9571, 10.8033).

Surface : **Gravel**
Spaces : **>10**
Length : **>12**

36 Raubern

📍 59.4153, 9.7482

Photo: Tor Nordahl, ReiseMedia AS

Large grass campingsite with room for many cars and caravans if you use a little common sense. Bench and table are on the site. Several other sites in the area, see (59.4140, 9.7472)

Surface : **Gras**
Spaces : **>10**
Length : **>12**

37 Røskestadvannet

📍 59.5748, 10.5443

1778

Photo: Eivind Molde

A smaller site to free camp for small cars. If you have a big car or caravan you may park at (59.5740, 10.5449)

Surface : **Gravel**
Spaces : **2**
Length : **<8**

38 Storsand

📍 59.6572, 10.6037

1780

Photo: Góngora

Great sites at the tip of the breakwater. Several other possibilities at the marina just nearby. Also see parking at (59.6646, 10.6000)

Surface : **Gravel**
Spaces : **3**
Length : **<10**

39 Kongsberg

📍 59.6639, 9.6211

960

Photo: Fredno

Parking area in connection to the alpine resort.

Surface : **Gravel**
Spaces : **>20**
Length : **>12**

40 Nerdammen

📍 59.7961, 10.0785

170

Photo: Tor Nordahl, ReiseMedia AS

Large parking lot. Great place for hiking. You do not have to walk long befor you reach the path- and ski trail. There may be many cars here on weekends and holidays. Fishing licence can be purchased on www.inatur.no

Surface : **Gravel**
Spaces : **>10**
Length : **>12**

41 Litmovatnet Vest

📍 59.9273, 9.5841

368

Photo: Tor Nordahl, ReiseMedia AS

Great site for fishing . Fishing licence can be purchased at Letmoliegårdene (59.9332, 9.5789)

Surface : **Gras**
Spaces : **2**
Length : **>12**

42 Litmolivatnet Øst

📍 59.9289, 9.5928

1870

Photo: Tor Nordahl, ReiseMedia AS

Idyll at the dam. Lovely view of Litmolivatnet, great fishing. Remember to purchase a fishing license.

Surface : **Gras**
Spaces : **2**
Length : **<10**

43 Vikersundbakken

📍 59.9386, 9.9986

1001

Photo: Carsten Wiehe

Parking in connection to the ski jump. Plenty of room in the summer, it can be cramped here during events in the winter.

Surface : **Gravel**
Spaces : **>20**
Length : **>12**

44 Lauvnesvannet

📍 59.9513, 9.5887

370

Photo: Tor Nordahl, ReiseMedia AS

Two gorgeous locations with good sun exposure, relatively flat. Fishing and swimming opportunities, great hiking options in the area. The site is close by the road, but there is almost no traffic.

Surface : **Gravel**
Spaces : **2**
Length : **<8**

45 Grytevatn

📍 60.0163, 9.4498

372

Photo: Tor Nordahl, ReiseMedia AS

Grass area with tables and great view overlokking Grytevatn.

Surface : **Gras**
Spaces : **3**
Length : **>12**

46 Moslontjenn

📍 60.0277, 9.4263

1658

Photo: Tor Nordahl, ReiseMedia AS

Small site next to the water.

Surface : **Gravel**
Spaces : **1**
Length : **<8**

47 Grunntjønn

📍 60.0453, 9.3905

1877

Photo: Tor Nordahl, ReiseMedia AS

Turnaround with room to launch boats in a cabin area. Room for 1-2 cars/caravans. Great views overlooking the water. Facilitated with benches and barbecue area.

Surface : **Gravel**
Spaces : **2**
Length : **<8**

48 Sandungen

📍 60.0494, 9.8996

175

Photo:Tor Nordahl, ReiseMedia AS

Site for fishing. Very quiet area! Also check (60.0447, 9.9087)

Surface : **Gravel**
Spaces : **1**
Length : **< 8**

49 Nedre Tråentjønn

📍 60.0562, 9.3745

373

Photo: Tor Nordahl, ReiseMedia AS

Great site (gravel) at the end of the road, several sites in this area. Excellent starting point for hikes in Trillemarka-Rollagsfjell which is the largest natural forest-reserve in Norway.

Surface : **Gravel**
Spaces : **3**
Length : **<10**

50 Vilsamtjern

📍 60.1054, 9.8848

178

Photo: Tor Nordahl, ReiseMedia AS

Drive by way of Kløftefoss (60.0885, 9.8337). Great place by the water. Near the western village of Deadwood City. Show every Sunday in the season in connection with the museum railway "Krødernbanen".

Surface : **Gravel**
Spaces : **4**
Length : **>10**

51 Damtjern

📍 60.1082, 9.8657

177

Photo:Tor Nordahl, ReiseMedia AS

At forest pond. A bit steep down towards the lakeside. Site is near the road although there is almost no traffic. You may camp on the road that is no longer in use just inside the forest.

Surface : **Gravel**
Spaces : **3**
Length : **>10**

52 Røsholmstranda

📍 60.1227, 10.1897

163

Photo: Tor Nordahl, ReiseMedia AS

Parking lot to the beach. Recreational area with lawn and kiosk during the season. A lot of people when the weather is nice during the season.

Surface : **Gras**
Spaces : **>10**
Length : **>12**

53 Norefjell

📍 60.2179, 9.5664

973

Photo: Bjoertvedt

Suitable for free camping in the summer. Space for several cars at this site and you may have to pay a parking fee in the winter.

Surface : **Gravel**
Spaces : **>10**
Length : **>12**

54 Uvdal Alpinsenter

📍 60.3010, 8.5385

996

Photo: Tor Nordahl, ReiseMedia AS

Large parking lot at the alpine resort.

Surface : **Gravel**
Spaces : **>20**
Length : **>12**

55 Høgevarde Fjellpark

📍 60.3391, 9.5046

Photo: Bjoertvedt

Gravel parking in connection to the alpine resort. Great starting point for hikes in the summer.

Surface : **Gravel**
Spaces : **>10**
Length : **>12**

56 Haglebu skisenter

📍 60.3449, 9.1902

Photo: Jan-Tore Egge

Parking in connection to the alpine resort. There are several campsites in the area if you need facilities.

Surface : **Gravel**
Spaces : **>10**
Length : **>12**

57 Dagali

📍 60.3960, 8.4251

Photo: Tor Nordahl, ReiseMedia AS

Large parking lot by the alpine resort. Picnic area with showers and you may empty your chemical toilets at (60.4071, 8.4400).

Surface : **Gravel**
Spaces : **>20**
Length : **>12**

58 Fagerheim

📍 60.4393, 7.7956

A small place along the road. There are several opportunities in the area. Eg (60.4387, 7.8100) - (60.4386, 7.8084) - (60.4366, 7.7827) and (60.4351, 7.7734). You can also park on Fagerheim Fjellstugu (60.4394, 7.7861)

Surface : **Gravel**
Spaces : **2**
Length : **<12**

59 Geilo

📍 60.5230, 8.1998

Photo: Tor Nordahl, ReiseMedia AS

Large parking lot at the alpine and mountain resort. Several opportunities in the area - also check (60.5456, 8.1999) and (60.5340, 8.1998) - Service area just off the site at (60.5266, 8.2160)

Surface : **Gravel**
Spaces : **>20**
Length : **>12**

60 Embretstøltjørni

📍 60.5261, 7.9564

Photo: WikiCommons

Large gravel excursion parking at the end of the road. Several opportunities along the road that leads up to this site. Toll road. You need cash for paying, you leave the money in an envelope in a box at site.

Surface : **Gravel**
Spaces : **>10**
Length : **<10**

61 Nesbyen Alpin/Golf

📍 60.5334, 9.0285

Photo: Tor Nordahl, ReiseMedia AS

Large parking lot by the alpine resort.

Surface	:	**Gravel**
Spaces	:	**>50**
Length	:	**>12**

62 Hallingskarvet

📍 60.6469, 8.0283

Photo: Tor Nordahl, ReiseMedia AS

Large parking lot at the alpine resort.

Surface	:	**Gravel**
Spaces	:	**>20**
Length	:	**>12**

63 Ål Skisenter

📍 60.6684, 8.5359

Photo: Tor Nordahl, ReiseMedia AS

Large gravel parking at the alpine resort.

Surface	:	**Gravel**
Spaces	:	**>10**
Length	:	**>12**

64 Gol – Skagahøgdi Skisenter

📍 60.7088, 8.9174

Photo: Chell Hill

Close to Gol church.

Surface	:	**Gravel**
Spaces	:	**<5**
Length	:	**<10**

65 Rauddalsvatnet

📍 60.7170, 9.2831

Photo: Frankemann

Gravel sites at Rauddalsvatnet, suitable for free camping. Also check (60.7162, 9.2848)

Surface	:	**Gravel**
Spaces	:	**>5**
Length	:	**>12**

66 Storefjell

📍 60.8045, 8.9531

Photo: Tor Nordahl, ReiseMedia AS

Parking lot behind Storefjell hotel.

Surface	:	**Asphalt**
Spaces	:	**>10**
Length	:	**>12**

67 Golsfjellet – Bualie

📍 60.8262, 8.9879

944

Photo: Tor Nordahl, ReiseMedia AS

Large gravel parking lot for the ski center. Nice view to Tisleifjorden. Nice starting point for bicycle tours. Toll road NOK. 40, -

Surface : **Gravel**
Spaces : **>20**
Length : **>12**

68 Hemsedal

📍 60.8630, 8.5200

954

Photo: Tor Nordahl, ReiseMedia AS

Large parking lot, short distance to afterski and ski lift. Can be a lot of people in the winter season.

Surface : **Gravel**
Spaces : **>20**
Length : **>12**

Free Campers

• GUIDE TO NORWAY 2019 •

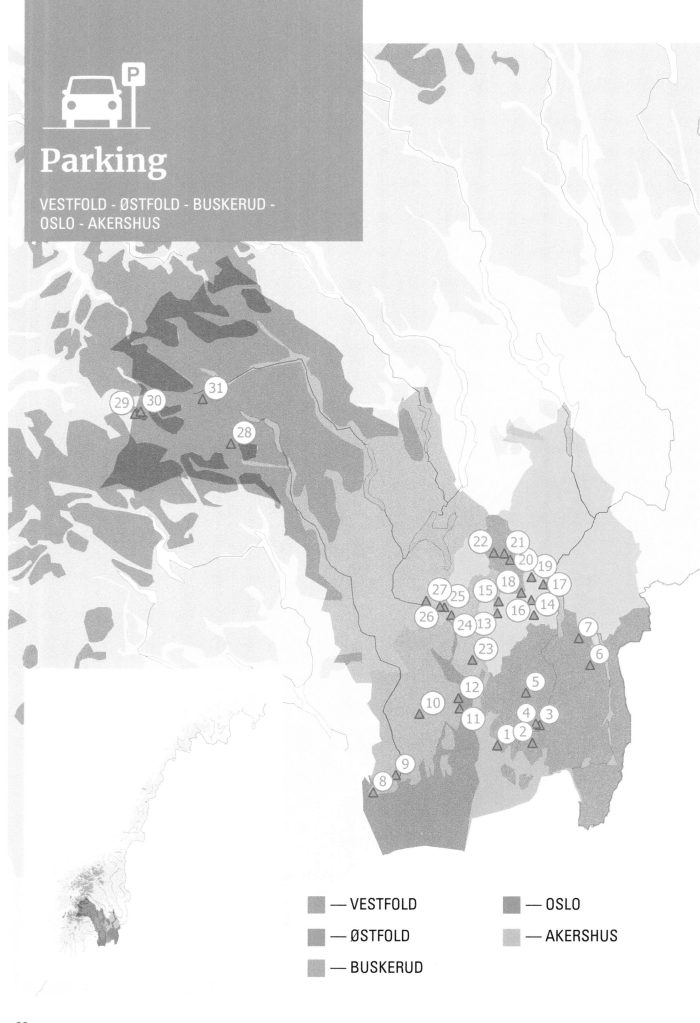

Parking

VESTFOLD - ØSTFOLD - BUSKERUD - OSLO - AKERSHUS

— VESTFOLD
— ØSTFOLD
— BUSKERUD
— OSLO
— AKERSHUS

1 Mærrapanna

📍 59.1973, 10.7962

Photo: T. Schrøder

Large gravel parking lot at the nature reserve and the recreational area.

Surface : **Gravel**
Spaces : **>10**
Length : **>12**

2 Skjærvik/Vispen

📍 59.2162, 11.0689

Photo: Andrej Tanusha

Parking at the swimming area / recreation area

Surface : **Gravel**
Spaces : **3**
Length : **<10**

3 Glengshølen

📍 59.2885, 11.1172

Parking at the recreation area

Surface : **Gravel**
Spaces : **5**
Length : **>12**

4 Tunevannet

📍 59.2934, 11.0869

Foto:Olaf Mørkeseth

Large car park at the swimming area. Diving tower, toilets and kiosk. Known for fine fishing opportunities.

Surface : **Asphalt**
Spaces : **>10**
Length : **>10**

5 Sæbyvannet

📍 59.4183, 10.9939

Photo: Tor Nordahl, ReiseMedia AS

Parking lot modelboat-track . Can be crowded on weekends in the summer when the weather is nice.

Surface : **Gravel**
Spaces : **>5**
Length : **>12**

6 Lundebyvannet Badeplass

📍 59.5462, 11.4828

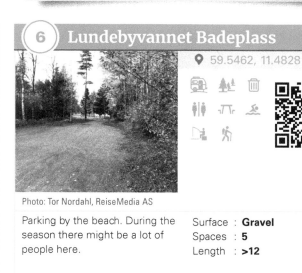

Photo: Tor Nordahl, ReiseMedia AS

Parking by the beach. During the season there might be a lot of people here.

Surface : **Gravel**
Spaces : **5**
Length : **>12**

7 Dilleviktårnet

📍 59.6527, 11.3819

225

Photo: Tor Nordahl, ReiseMedia AS

Parking at the nature reserve / protected area.

Surface : **Gravel**
Spaces : **2**
Length : **<8**

8 Nevlunghavn

📍 58.9730, 9.8631

274

Photo: Winifred

Large municipal parking. Free.

Surface : **Asphalt**
Spaces : **>50**
Length : **>12**

9 Larvik Havn

📍 59.0503, 10.0267

281

Free parking for motorhomes up to 48 hours. Also check motorhome parking with facilities at 59.0489, 10.0335

Surface : **Asphalt**
Spaces : **4**
Length : **<10**

10 Andebu

📍 59.3038, 10.1741

307

Photo: Mahlum

Open site 200 meters from the city center.

Surface : **Asphalt**
Spaces : **>10**
Length : **>12**

11 Åsgårstrand

📍 59.3370, 10.4850

309

Photo: Michal Hope

Large parking at the swimming area / recreation area

Surface :
Spaces :
Length :

12 Steinbrygga båthavn

📍 59.3787, 10.4692

310

Photo: Kurth Brekke

Recreational area / National Park. You may empty the toilet at the family camping site close by. You should use the campsite in the season.

Surface : **Gravel**
Spaces : **>10**
Length : **>12**

13 Breivoll friområde

📍 59.7354, 10.7285

Photo: Tor Nordahl, ReiseMedia AS

Large recreational area with swimming, soccer and hiking trails. Parking facilities along the road. (59.7341, 10.7294) and (59.7313, 10.7309).

Surface : **Gravel**
Spaces : **>20**
Length : **>12**

14 Våg – Ytre Enebakk

📍 59.7374, 11.0192

Photo: pvang

Large gravel parking in connection with the swimming area.

Surface : **Gravel**
Spaces : **>10**
Length : **>10**

15 Svartskog Brygge

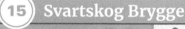

📍 59.7852, 10.7330

Photo: Øyvind Arntsen

Parking lot located directly at Roald Amundsen's home in Svartskog. Is best suited for small cars and are not suitable for caravans.

Surface : **Beton**
Spaces : **2**
Length : **<6**

16 Bysetermåsan

📍 59.7987, 10.9912

Photo: Tor Nordahl, ReiseMedia AS

Parking. Great base for hiking in Østmarka on skis or on foot

Surface : **Gravel**
Spaces : **>5**
Length : **>12**

17 Myrdammen

📍 59.8655, 11.0795

Photo: Tor Nordahl, ReiseMedia AS

Large parking lot at the swimming and recreation area

Surface : **Gravel**
Spaces : **>10**
Length : **>12**

18 Setertjern

📍 59.8265, 10.9082

Photo: Tor Nordahl, ReiseMedia AS

Large parking lot for hiking in Østmarka

Surface : **Asphalt**
Spaces : **>20**
Length : **>12**

19 Losby

⌖ 59.8920, 10.9812

Photo: Tor Nordahl, ReiseMedia AS

Greate parking facilities at Østmarka. Also check (59.8916, 10.9750) - (59.8878, 10.9813) - Max 72 hours

Surface : **Asphalt**
Spaces : **>20**
Length : **>12**

20 Grefsenkollen

⌖ 59.9569, 10.8028

Foto: Tor Nordahl, ReiseMedia AS.

Large parking lot at the top of Oslo - View point close by. Restaurant at the top and at Trollvann. Swimming area at Trollvann.

Surface : **Gravel**
Spaces : **>20**
Length : **>12**

21 Maridalen

⌖ 59.9811, 10.7530

Photo: Tor Nordahl, ReiseMedia AS

Large parking lot for walks in the woods around Oslo

Surface : **Gravel**
Spaces : **>20**
Length : **>12**

22 Tryvann

⌖ 59.9816, 10.6694

Photo:Tor Nordahl, ReiseMedia AS

Multiple parking lots actually ment for skiing tourists but it`s also useable in the summertime. A lot of motorhomes park here.
The lake is very cold but you can swim in it. Tram station for access to Oslo nearby.

Surface : **Asphalt**
Spaces : **>50**
Length : **>12**

23 Tofte

⌖ 59.5394, 10.5581

Photo: Helge Høifødt

Large gravel parking lot on odd in Tofte center.

Surface : **Gravel**
Spaces : **>10**
Length : **<12**

24 Hyggen

⌖ 59.7163, 10.3674

Photo: Bkv

Parking by the beach. Can be crowded on sunny days during the swimming season. Also try at the marina at (59.7148, 10.3639)

Surface : **Gravel**
Spaces : **5**
Length : **<12**

25 Gullaug

📍 59.7471, 10.3071

Photo: Jan-Tore Egge

Quiet parking place at colsed down railway route. Great hiking inward Kjekstadmarka. Suitable only for smaller cars.

Surface : **Gravel**
Spaces : **5**
Length : **<7**

26 Linnesstranda

📍 59.7479, 10.2714

Photo: Raimon Bjørndalen

Quiet parking space with recreational and swimming area. Nature reserve.

Surface : **Asphalt**
Spaces : **>5**
Length : **<10**

27 Landfalltjern

📍 59.7687, 10.1603

Photo: Tor Nordahl, ReiseMedia AS

Recreational and swimming area with large parking lot.

Surface : **Asphalt**
Spaces : **>20**
Length : **>10m**

28 Vasstulan

📍 60.3386, 8.4971

Parking on both sides of the road. Plenty of room for parking in the summertime., not som much in the winter. Toilets when the cafe is open.

Surface : **Gravel**
Spaces : **>10**
Length : **>12**

29 Halne rasteplass

📍 60.4181, 7.7049

Photo: Christoffer H. Støle

Large paved parking along the road. Amazing view.

Surface : **Asphalt**
Spaces : **>5**
Length : **>12**

30 Båtstjørne rasteplass

📍 60.4297, 7.7487

Photo: Roger Ellingsen/Statens vegvesen

Gravel parking lot with views

Surface : **Gravel**
Spaces : **3**
Length : **>12**

31 Geilotjørne

⦿ 60.5061, 8.2344

397

Photo: Graham Lewis

Large parking lot

Surface : **Gravel**
Spaces : **>15**
Length : **>12**

• GUIDE TO NORWAY 2019 •

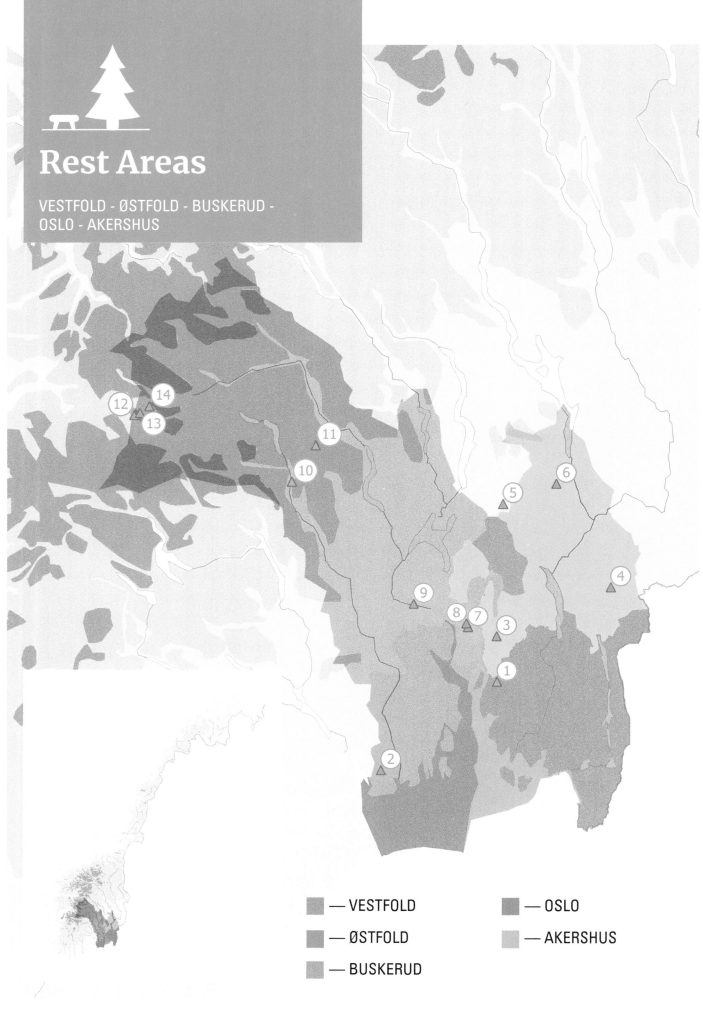

Rest Areas

VESTFOLD - ØSTFOLD - BUSKERUD -
OSLO - AKERSHUS

■ — VESTFOLD

■ — ØSTFOLD

■ — BUSKERUD

■ — OSLO

■ — AKERSHUS

1 Rødsund rasteplass

📍 59.4616, 10.7681

155

Photo: Tor Nordahl, ReiseMedia AS

Nice picnic area with opportunities for swimming in Vansjø

Surface : **Asphalt**
Spaces : **>5**
Length : **>12**

2 Vassbotn

📍 59.0725, 9.9153

283

Large picnic area on both sides of the road. Kiosk and takeaways.

Surface : **Asphalt**
Spaces : **>20**
Length : **>12**

3 Ås

📍 59.6467, 10.7412

334

Picnic area for trucks

Surface : **Asphalt**
Spaces : **>20**
Length : **>12**

4 Bjørkelangen

📍 59.8755, 11.6203

84

Photo: Tor Nordahl, ReiseMedia AS

Picnic area with swimming possibilities.

Surface : **Asphalt**
Spaces : **<10**
Length : **>12**

5 Harestuvatnet

📍 60.1881, 10.7221

1738

Photo: Tor Nordahl, ReiseMedia AS

Recreational area down towards the water. Great for swimming and fishing but a little close to the road even though there is very little traffic. Can be cramped for space on fine summer days.

Surface : **Gravel**
Spaces : **3**
Length : **>12**

6 Andelva rasteplass

📍 60.2825, 11.1389

378

Photo: Tor Nordahl, ReiseMedia AS

Waste disposal points for motorhomes and caravans. Rest areas in both the northbound and southbound direction.

Surface : **Asphalt**
Spaces : **>20**
Length : **>12**

7 Sætre sør

📍 59.6763, 10.5109

337

Picnic area.

Surface : **Asphalt**
Spaces : **>20**
Length : **>12**

8 Sætre nord

📍 59.6911, 10.4960

339

Picnic area

Surface : **Asphalt**
Spaces : **>20**
Length : **>12**

9 Herstrøm rasteplass

📍 59.7584, 10.0692

345

Photo: Stian Martinsen

Large picnic area. Toilets and picnic tables. Drammenselva runs close by. Idyllic but a lot of traffic.

Surface : **Asphalt**
Spaces : **>10**
Length : **>12**

10 Raustand

📍 60.2122, 9.0199

377

Photo : J.P.Fagerback

Picnic area with trash cans and picnic tables. Also see small exit at 60.2165, 9.0176 where there is room for a camper or caravan.

Surface : **Gravel**
Spaces : **3**
Length : **<10**

11 Bergsætra

📍 60.3684, 9.1851

1760

Overview Eggerdal. Photo: Helge Høifødt

Gravel picnic area. Good starting point for hikes.

Surface : **Gravel**
Spaces : **5**
Length : **>12**

12 Halne rasteplass

📍 60.4181, 7.7049

388

Photo: Christoffer H. Støle

Large paved parking along the road. Amazing view.

Surface : **Asphalt**
Spaces : **>5**
Length : **>12**

13 Båtstjørne rasteplass

📍 60.4297, 7.7487

Photo: Roger Ellingsen/Statens vegvesen

Gravel parking lot with views

Surface : **Gravel**
Spaces : **3**
Length : **>12**

14 Lægreidstølen

📍 60.4614, 7.8180

Photo: Sergey Ashmarin

Large gravel picnic area

Surface : **Gravel**
Spaces : **>5**
Length : **>12**

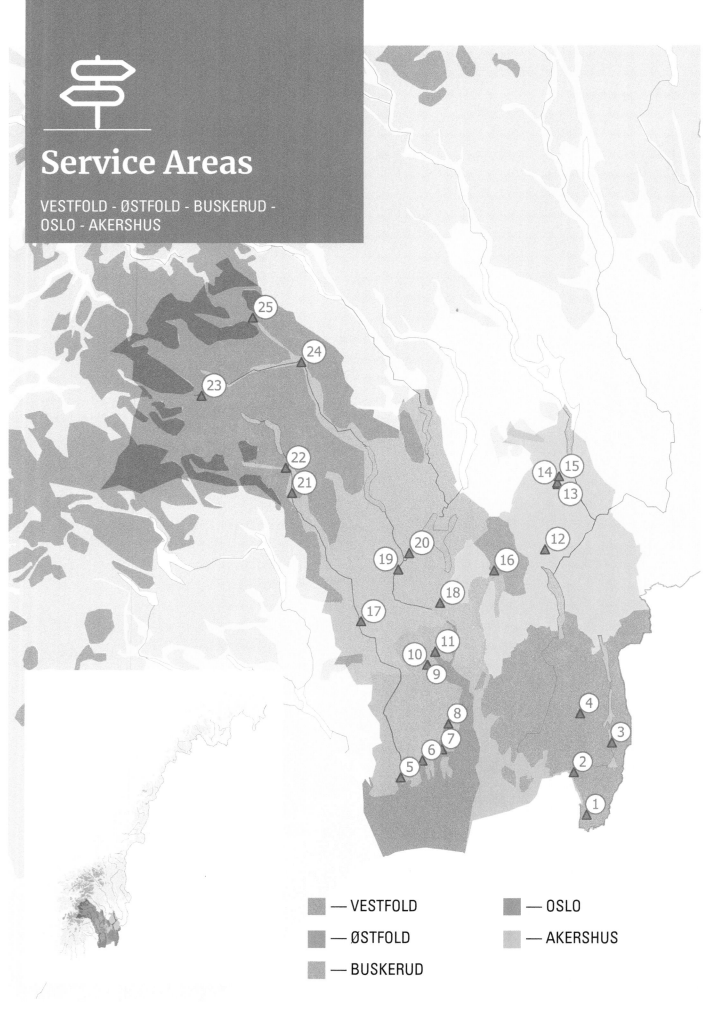

Service Areas

VESTFOLD - ØSTFOLD - BUSKERUD -
OSLO - AKERSHUS

— VESTFOLD

— ØSTFOLD

— BUSKERUD

— OSLO

— AKERSHUS

1 Svenningsbø
📍 58.9477, 11.5163

Enningdalen

1191

2 Halden
📍 59.1154, 11.3983

At the entrance at Fredriksten camping, Generalveien 16

1192

3 Kirkeng
📍 59.2418, 11.6825

Kirkeng camping just south of Aremark church

1190

4 Degernes
📍 59.3533, 11.4222

Best. Clean water, open all day. Free.

1193

5 Larvik
📍 59.0504, 10.0620

Esso, Elveveien 21

1160

6 Sandefjord
📍 59.1249, 10.2205

Shell and motorhome port

1164

7 Tenvik
📍 59.1745, 10.3651

The pier in Tenvik, also for boats.

1161

8 Tønsberg
📍 59.2792, 10.4006

Shell

1162

9 Grelland - Nord
📍 59.5142, 10.2044

Circle K E-18 north

1159

10 Grelland - Sør
📍 59.5143, 10.2015

Shell E-18 south

1158

11 Selvik
📍 59.5695, 10.2552

Lersbrygga wastewater treatment plant.

1163

12 Berger
📍 60.0153, 11.0690

Berger, outside commercial building (former Oslo Caravan). Winter Open.

1194

13 Andelva - Sør
📍 60.2824, 11.1388

Picnic area

1195

14 Andelva - Nord
📍 60.2892, 11.1340

Picnic area

1196

15 Nebbenes
📍 60.3147, 11.1453

Shell, on the northbound side, take the bridge over the road if you are going southbound.

1197

16 Oslo - Sjølyst
📍 59.9180, 10.6755

Sjølyst motorhome parking, June 1st - September 15th.

1198

17 Kongsberg
📍 59.6710, 9.6548

Shell Express.

1202

18 Lier
📍 59.7717, 10.2652

Circle K, slightly tucked away right at the entrance at the station. GPS coordinates are accurate.

1203

19 Kongsfoss
📍 59.8948, 9.9156

Åmot on RV287

1205

20 Vikersund
📍 59.9638, 9.99207

Øya pumping station

1204

21 Nore
📍 60.1681, 9.01803

YX

1206

22 Rødberg
📍 60.2676, 8.94976

Recycling Center?

1207

23 Geilo
📍 60.5263, 8.2157

Geilo - Stølsvegen 32. The exit towards Vestlia from FV 40. Follow the signs from downtown.

1201

24 Gol
📍 60.7009, 8.99554

Wastewater treatment plant just east of downtown Gol.

1199

25 Hemsedal
📍 60.8613, 8.56699

East from the council house, about 1 km from Trøim center.

1200

VESTFOLD - ØSTFOLD - BUSKERUD - OSLO - AKERSHUS

Oppland

Oppland is a county bordering Trøndelag, Møre og Romsdal, Sogn og Fjordane, Buskerud, Akershus, Oslo and Hedmark. The county administration is in Lillehammer. Oppland is, together with Hedmark, one of the only two landlocked counties of Norway. The largest cities in Oppland are Lillehammer, Gjøvik, Raufoss, Brandbu/Jaren, Jevnaker, Dokka, Vinstra and Fagernes. Population (2017) = 189.870

Hedmark

Hedmark makes up the northeastern part of Østlandet, the southeastern part of the country. It has a long border with Sweden, Dalarna County and Värmland County. The largest lakes are Femunden and Mjøsa, the largest lake in Norway. Parts of Glomma, Norway's longest river, flow through Hedmark. Geographically, Hedmark is traditionally divided into: Hedemarken, east of Mjøsa, Østerdalen, north of Elverum, and Glåmdalen, south of Elverum. Hedmark and Oppland are the only Norwegian counties with no coastline. Hedmark also hosted some events of the 1994 Winter Olympic Games. The largest cities in Hedmark are Hamar, Elverum, Kongsvinger, Brummundal, Bekkelaget, Moelv, Stange, Løten og Tynset. Population (2017) = 196.966

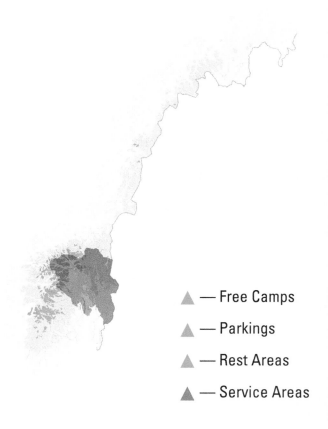

▲ — Free Camps

▲ — Parkings

▲ — Rest Areas

▲ — Service Areas

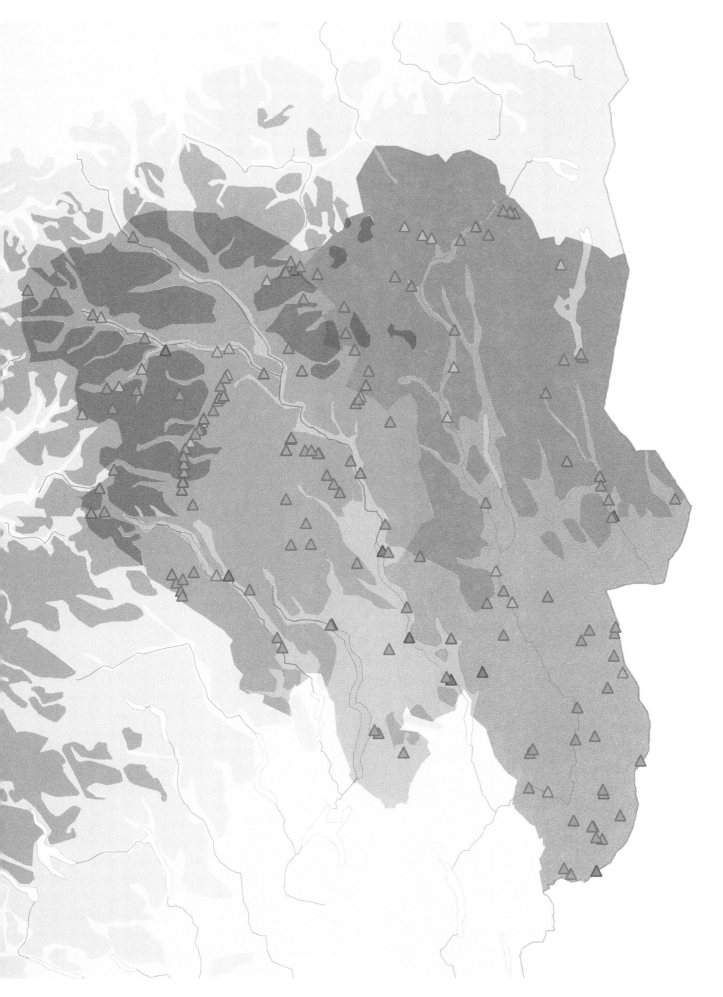

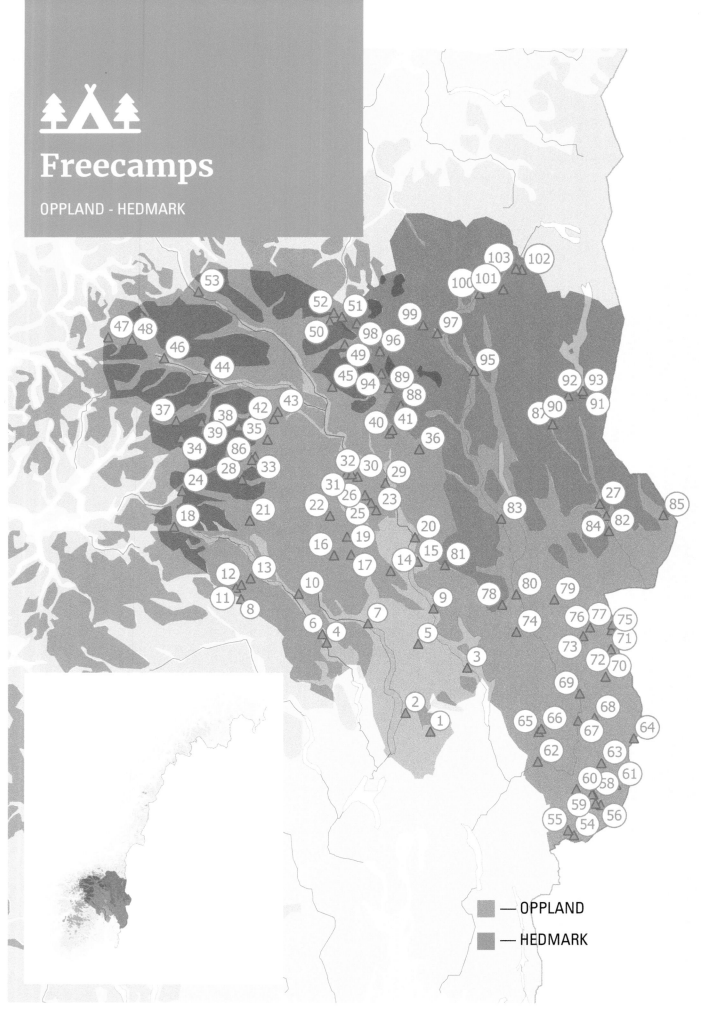

Freecamps

OPPLAND - HEDMARK

OPPLAND

HEDMARK

1 Våja

📍 60.3485, 10.7108

Photo: Tor Nordahl, ReiseMedia AS

Lovely area for free camping. Several large sites along the quiet road. See (60.3460, 10.7104) and (60.3472, 10.7087)

Surface : **Gravel**
Spaces : **>20**
Length : **>12**

2 Røykenvika

📍 60.4274, 10.4763

Photo: Jan-Tore Egge

Recreational area next to the museum. Many opportunities in the area. Such as (60.4279, 10.4751)

Surface : **Gras**
Spaces : **>10**
Length : **>12**

3 Panengen Brygge

📍 60.6515, 11.0073

Photo: Øyvind Holmstad

Large recreational area with swimming opportunities, kiosk and picnic tables. There may be a lot of people here during the summer season, on sunny days and weekends.

Surface : **Gravel**
Spaces : **>5**
Length : **>12**

4 Eid kraftverk

📍 60.7209, 9.7132

Photo: PeltonMan

Below or just next to dam

Surface : **Gravel**
Spaces : **5**
Length : **>12**

5 Skumsjøen

📍 60.7455, 10.5463

Photo: Eivind Molde

A great place with several possibilities for lodging with motorhome, camper and tents. No facility service, but close to a large DNT cabin (The Norwegian Trekking Association).

Surface : **Gravel**
Spaces : **>5**
Length : **<10**

6 Fønhus

📍 60.7582, 9.6666

Photo: Jon Erling Blad

Wonderfull site (gravel) down by the river. Recreational area with picnic tables, this site is also used as a camp for fishing.

Surface : **Gravel**
Spaces : **4**
Length : **<10**

7 Dokka

📍 60.8233, 10.0743

Photo: Øyvind Holmstad

Small gravel site used as a base for fishing in the river Etna

Surface : **Gravel**
Spaces : **2**
Length : **<10**

8 Tisleivegen

📍 60.8893, 8.8952

Photo: H.-N. Meiforth

Idyllic site in the cottage area down towards the river Flya. Also see (60.8875, 8.8967)

Surface : **Gravel**
Spaces : **5**
Length : **<10**

9 Biri

📍 60.9135, 10.6626

Photo: Torstein

Recreational area, beach with swimming opportunities. Remains of an old industry, but neat and tidy down by the pier. It might look like it`s a private area, but as you follow the road past the house then you will reach the public outdoor recreation area.

Surface : **Gravel**
Spaces : **>5**
Length : **<10**

10 Valdres Alpinsenter, Aurdal

📍 60.9361, 9.4178

Photo: Kimmert

Large parking area in connection to the alpine resort.

Surface : **Gravel**
Spaces : **>20**
Length : **>12**

11 Haugvarpet

📍 60.9385, 8.8378

Photo: Norheim

Area with boat ramp, here you will find large gravel and grass camping sites for free. Great view over the Storfjord.

Surface : **Gravel**
Spaces : **>10**
Length : **>10**

12 Reinsennvatnet

📍 60.9539, 8.8861

Photo: Erlend Bjoertvedt

Large recreational area down towards the water.

Surface : **Gravel**
Spaces : **>10**
Length : **>10**

13 Vaset skiheiser

📍 60.9866, 8.9661

Photo: Tor Nordahl, ReiseMedia AS

Parking in connection to the ski lift.

Surface : **Gravel**
Spaces : **>10**
Length : **<10**

14 Sjoga

📍 61.0727, 10.2464

Photo: Lillehammer Kommune

Small side road down to the water. Not suitable for big cars or caravans.

Surface : **Gravel**
Spaces : **2**
Length : **<8**

15 Lysgårdsbakken

📍 61.1233, 10.4869

Photo: pa.jus

Large gravel parking at the sports complex

Surface :
Spaces : **>20**
Length : **>12**

16 Røssjørompa

📍 61.1242, 9.7131

Photo: Jan-Tore Egge

Grassy area well suited for freecamping. Picnic table and path down to the water. Also check the rest area at (61.1242, 9.7204) where there is room for many cars over a larger area.

Surface : **Gras**
Spaces : **4**
Length : **>12**

17 Spåtind

📍 61.1330, 9.8702

Photo: Jan Arne Ekkeren

Parking lot.

Surface : **Gravel**
Spaces : **>10**
Length : **>12**

18 Filefjell skisenter, Tyin

📍 61.1887, 8.2163

Photo: karlosluz

Parking lot in connection to the alpine resort. Nice site to park in the summer, can be a lot of cars during weekends and hollidays in the winter. Try also free camp at (61.1807, 8.2095) in the summer.

Surface : **Gravel**
Spaces : **>20**
Length : **>12**

19 Dokkvatn S

📍 61.2139, 9.8185

435

Great recreational area down by the water. Sandy beach.

Surface : **Gras**
Spaces : **2**
Length : **<8**

20 Hafjell

📍 61.2333, 10.4474

948

Photo: Hafjell

Parking in connection to the alpine resort.

Surface : **Gravel**
Spaces : **>20**
Length : **>12**

21 Beitostølen

📍 61.2496, 8.9076

924

Photo: larsonk

Parking in connection to the alpine resort.

Surface : **Gravel**
Spaces : **>20**
Length : **>12**

22 Øvre Ongsøen

📍 61.3026, 9.6447

437

Photo: Sonnenscheinbs

Site on the odd out towards Øvre Ongsjøen. More possibilities in the area (61.3023, 9.6531) and (61.3015, 9.6452)

Surface : **Gras**
Spaces : **3**
Length : **>12**

23 Gausdal – Skeikampen

📍 61.3449, 10.0684

940

Photo: Aconcagua

Large grave site used for car parking. Several other cars in the winter, but plenty of room in the summer.

Surface : **Gravel**
Spaces : **>100**
Length : **>12**

24 Tyinholmen

📍 61.3548, 8.2563

1704

Photo: Tore Umes

Site with great views down towards the water. Restaurant on Tyinholmen, season mid-June to early October.

Surface : **Gravel**
Spaces : **>5**
Length : **<10**

25 Massingtjønna

📍 61.3759, 10.0141

833

Photo: Aconcagua

Several great sites around the pond. Toll road NOK 80, - but well worth the money! Great area for walking. More great sites along the road. See (61.3926, 9.9779).

Surface :	**Gras**
Spaces :	**>10**
Length :	**>10**

26 Pallbu

📍 61.4089, 9.9529

834

Photo: Aconcagua

Large parking lot just of the road. Great area for hiking. Drinking water and café at Fagerhøy where there also is parking. http://www.fagerhoi.no/en/Mountain-Lodge

Surface :	**Gravel**
Spaces :	**<10**
Length :	**>12**

27 Jordet

📍 61.4322, 12.1462

447

Photo: Einar Fredriksen

Large areas along Trysilelva

Surface :	**Gravel**
Spaces :	**>10**
Length :	**>10**

28 Flybekken

📍 61.4331, 8.7974

448

Photo: Werner Harstad/Statens vegvesen

Large recreational area near small picnic area.

Surface :	**Gravel**
Spaces :	**>10**
Length :	**>12**

29 Kvitfjell

📍 61.4718, 10.1357

961

Photo: przemcio

Large gravel site used as parking at the alpine resort. Great for free camping in the summer. Many other possibilities such as (61.4909, 10.1146) and (61.4913, 10.1287)

Surface :	**Gravel**
Spaces :	**>10**
Length :	**>12**

30 Nordrelia

📍 61.4905, 9.8695

1752

Photo: Jan Hammershaug

Just off the road. Great site for spending the night.

Surface :	**Gras**
Spaces :	**3**
Length :	**<12**

31 Gåla Arena

📍 61.4972, 9.7644

456

Photo: Øyvind Holmstad

Large parking lot in connection to the ski arena.

Surface : **Gravel**
Spaces : **>20**
Length : **>12**

32 Storstultjønna

📍 61.5001, 9.8138

1751

Photo: Gammel'n

Slightly off the road. Great views on top of the hill.

Surface : **Gras**
Spaces : **3**
Length : **<10**

33 Sjodalsvatnet

📍 61.5422, 8.9010

464

Photo: Peter Bouwmeester

Picnic area/recreational area down by the water

Surface : **Gravel**
Spaces : **3**
Length : **<10**

34 Leirvassbuvegen

📍 61.5931, 8.1930

1709

Photo: Frankemann

There are several great sites along the road. The coordinates show parking for hikes to Storbrean. There are several great sites such as (61.6131, 8.1782) and (61.6423, 8.1757) which are suitable for free camping.

Surface : **Gravel**
Spaces : **>10**
Length : **<10**

35 Steinhølet

📍 61.6238, 9.0013

474

Photo: Silver

Recreational area suitable for camping. Starting point for rafting. Great fishing.

Surface : **Gras**
Spaces : **>20**
Length : **>12**

36 Ringebufjellet – Åsdalstjørna

📍 61.6350, 10.4290

159

Photo: Lipo

Large area with beautiful views of Åsdalstjønna. Several places to stay with motorhome along Friisvegen (FV385).

Surface : **Gravel**
Spaces : **>10**
Length : **>12**

37 Høydalsvatnet

📍 61.6683, 8.1294

Photo: Frankemann

Several locations close to the water. Great starting point for hikes.

Surface : **Gras**
Spaces : **>5**
Length : **<10**

38 Glitterheim

📍 61.6715, 8.7187

Photo: Sondrekv

Parking for hiking to Glitterheim (61.6229, 8.6330) or Glittertind, Norway's second highest mountain at 2460m. Toll road.

Surface : **Gravel**
Spaces : **>10**
Length : **<10**

39 Juvasshytta

📍 61.6732, 8.3694

Photo: Harald Hooghiemstra

Excellent free camp with several sites in the area, also outside the parking lot. Summer-ski May to November. Starting point for trips up to Galdhøpiggen which is Northern Europe's highest mountain 2.469m

Surface : **Gravel**
Spaces : **>20**
Length : **>12**

40 Bølvatnet

📍 61.6969, 10.1385

Photo: Inatur

Several great sites along the gravel road towards Bølvatnet and Langrumpa.

Surface : **Gravel**
Spaces : **>10**
Length : **>10**

41 Muvatnet

📍 61.7138, 10.1623

Photo: Jarle Wæhler/Statens vegvesen

Large gravel sites off the road. Lots of opportunities in the area. National tourist route.

Surface : **Gravel**
Spaces : **>20**
Length : **>10**

42 Randsverk

📍 61.7207, 9.0403

Photo: Zairon

Gravel site down toward a small river. Toll road.

Surface : **Gravel**
Spaces : **2**
Length : **<10**

43 Lemonsjøen

📍 61.7545, 9.0715

Large gravel parking lot used for parking at the alpine resort. Great to free camp in the summer, but can be a lot of cars and traffic in teh winter

Surface : **Gravel**
Spaces : **>20**
Length : **>12**

44 Anstadøye

📍 61.8775, 8.3937

Photo: Zairon

Gravel site surrounded by trees.

Surface : **Gravel**
Spaces : **<10**
Length : **>12**

45 Høvringsvatne

📍 61.8896, 9.5649

Photo: Sverdrup

Great site out towards Høvringsvatne. Great starting point for hikes. There are parking facilitated for motorhomes at (61.8907, 9.5656)

Surface : **Gravel**
Spaces :
Length :

46 Stamåsagi

📍 61.9471, 7.9517

Photo: Musca Ro

Recreational area well suited for free camping. Holds a lot of cars, caravans and tents.

Surface : **Gravel**
Spaces : **>10**
Length : **<10**

47 Langvatnet

📍 62.0135, 7.4020

Photo: rdaniel

Large picnic area with opportunities for free camping at a distance from the rest area.

Surface : **Gravel**
Spaces : **>10**
Length : **>12**

48 Grotli

📍 62.0141, 7.6286

Photo: Aconcagua

Great parking in connection to the winter sports resort. Also see picnic area at (62.0144, 7.6214) and parking lot at (62.0100, 7.6269) but this can be closed during the summer.

Surface : **Gravel**
Spaces : **>20**
Length : **>12**

49 Grimsdalshytta

📍 62.0856, 9.6494

1905

Photo: Christer Gundersen

Large recreational area down towards the river. Great view and starting point for walks in the mountains

Surface : **Gras**
Spaces : **>20**
Length : **>12**

50 Sygardosen

📍 62.1851, 9.4869

1736

Photo: Frankemann

Great area with many opportunities for free camping or parking at rest area. Popular place in the summer, bu there is also room for several cars in the recreational area down towards Sygardosen and Burtjønne.

Surface : **Gravel**
Spaces : **>10**
Length : **>12**

51 Hjerkinnsdammen

📍 62.2111, 9.5998

1735

Hjerkinn Norway - Photo: Swedish National Heritage Board

Small site with views overlooking Hjerkindammen

Surface : **Gravel**
Spaces : **3**
Length : **<10**

52 Snøhetta

📍 62.2267, 9.5185

503

Photo:CH/visitnorway.com

Toilets and bins. Follow signs from E6 at Hjerkinn. We recommend the tour to view point Snøhetta 1,5km of dirt track. See website.

Surface : **Gravel**
Spaces : **>10**
Length : **>12**

53 Bjorli

📍 62.2658, 8.2101

925

Photo: Jan-Tore Egge

Large parking lot at the alpine resort. Use Bjorli winter camp at (62.2644, 8.2126) in the winter.

Surface : **Gravel**
Spaces : **>10**
Length : **>12**

54 Helgesjøen

📍 59.9138, 12.0466

367

Photo: Tor Nordahl, ReiseMedia AS

Parking with possibility for swimming. Often used by both motorhomes and caravans.

Surface : **Gravel**
Spaces : **>10**
Length : **>12**

55 Vestmarka

📍 59.9351, 11.9932

Photo: Tor Nordahl, ReiseMedia AS

Large recreational area. Several sites, base for hiking from for example Vekterveien. Playground equipment, vollyball and soccer area.

Surface : **Gras**
Spaces : **>10**
Length : **>12**

56 Nordre Billingen

📍 60.0560, 12.2748

Photo: Tor Nordahl, ReiseMedia AS

Dirt road down towards the water. This siste can only take 1 motorhome under 7 meters. A little steep, you must use high leveling blocks. Very secluded and idyllic.

Surface : **Gravel**
Spaces : **1**
Length : **<7**

57 Baksjøen – Eidskog

📍 60.0609, 12.2276

Photo: Tor Nordahl, ReiseMedia AS

Gravel site at odd. Nice view of Baksjøen

Surface : **Gravel**
Spaces : **2-3**
Length : **< 10**

58 Søndre Øyungen

📍 60.1026, 12.2043

Photo: Tor Nordahl - ReiseMedia AS

Rest area along a quiet road. Camping is not allowed, so do not put out chairs and tables. Parking is ok. You may use the picnic area but you may not stay longer than 24 hours. There are fields for playing soccer and volleyball in the sand.

Surface : **Gravel**
Spaces : **5**
Length : **> 10m**

59 Øyungen

📍 60.1029, 12.1928

Photo:Tor Nordahl, ReiseMedia AS

Odd near the road - fire place. Close to Southern Øyungen where there is parking.

Surface : **Gravel**
Spaces : **2**
Length : **<8**

60 Sigernessjøen

📍 60.1227, 12.0498

Photo: Tor Nordahl, ReiseMedia AS

Picnic area with possibility for swimming. Large barbecue area, picnic tables and trashcans. Site is near a busy road.

Surface : **Gravel**
Spaces : **>8**
Length : **>12**

61 Merratjenn

📍 60.1503, 12.4061

Photo: Tor Nordahl, ReiseMedia AS

Gravel parking by dam. Powerplant = no swimming at the pond. Off the road which has very little traffic.

Surface : **Gravel**
Spaces : **3**
Length : **<12**

62 Damlitjenn - Skarnes

📍 60.2409, 11.6927

Photo: Tor Nordahl, ReiseMedia AS

Parking lot with picnic tables. Starting point for the nature trail around Damlitjennet.

Surface : **Gravel**
Spaces : **2**
Length : **< 10**

63 Fjellsjøen

📍 60.2465, 12.2639

Photo: Tor Nordahl, ReiseMedia AS

Large area (gravel) down to Fjellsjøen. Brilliant for free camping. Great place for fishing.

Surface : **Gravel**
Spaces : **>5**
Length : **<10**

64 Kalsjøen

📍 60.3642, 12.5471

Photo: Tor Nordahl, ReiseMedia AS

Turnaround at the end of the dirt road. Several secluded places. Also check (60.3746, 12.5332)

Surface : **Gravel**
Spaces : **4**
Length : **<10**

65 Kalvhella

📍 60.3750, 11.6863

Photo: Tor Nordahl, ReiseMedia AS

Parking at the swimming area by Austvatn in Storsjøen

Surface : **Asphalt**
Spaces : **>3**
Length : **<10**

66 Bakkefløyta

📍 60.3902, 11.7085

Photo: Tor Nordahl, ReiseMedia AS

Site at dams. Shelter and bonfire on site. Good starting point for tours. Drive up to the site via (60.3807, 11.6886) http://news. reisemedia.no/2018/01/05/bakkefloyta/

Surface : **Gravel**
Spaces : **3**
Length : **<12**

67 Kongshov

60.4354, 12.0368

Photo:Tor Nordahl, ReiseMedia AS

Site at the river with fishing opportunities. Only room for 1 car.

Surface : **Gravel**
Spaces : **1**
Length : **<10**

68 Vollstadvika

60.4518, 12.1852

Photo: MIKojan

Swimming area with great parking. Homemade sign say that camping is not allowed, but it is OK to park/stay overnight if you do not put out chairs and tables! Also see (60.4526, 12.1682)

Surface : **Gravel**
Spaces : **5**
Length : **>12**

69 Arneberg

60.5596, 12.0399

Photo:Tor Nordahl, ReiseMedia AS

Site with fishing possibilities down toward the river

Surface : **Gravel**
Spaces : **2**
Length : **<10**

70 Velta

60.6414, 12.2689

Photo: Tor Nordahl, ReiseMedia AS

Gravel area with information board and museum. Also check the swimming area at (60.6394, 12.2662)

Surface : **Gravel**
Spaces : **4**
Length : **>12**

71 Risbekk

60.7671, 12.3078

Photo: Tor Nordahl, ReiseMedia AS

Great campground down by the river. Shelter with a fire place.

Surface : **Gravel**
Spaces : **>5**
Length : **>12**

72 Mastvelta

60.7674, 12.3082

Photo: Tor Nordahl, ReiseMedia AS

Fishing area with shelter. Near a quiet road.

Surface : **Gravel**
Spaces : **2**
Length : **<10**

73 Holsjøen

📍 60.8213, 12.0477

Photo: Tor Nordahl, ReiseMedia AS

Access for camping. Swimming, sandy beach, boat, pier, campfire and shelter. Well suited for fishing

Surface : **Gravel**
Spaces : **>10**
Length : **>10**

74 Mosjøen

📍 60.8270, 11.4352

Gravel site well off the dirt road. Several other options in the area. Also check out (60.8187, 11.4522)

Surface : **Gravel**
Spaces : **3**
Length : **>12**

75 Haldammen

📍 60.8544, 12.3055

Photo: Tor Nordahl,ReiseMedia AS

Parking near dam and waterfalls. Free access to the cabin with fireplace and benches. Make sure to bring in dry firewood and tidy up when you leave the cabin.

Surface : **Gravel**
Spaces : **2**
Length : **10**

76 Abbortjernet

📍 60.8628, 12.1078

Photo: Tor Nordahl, ReiseMedia AS

Gravel turnaround at the end of the dirt road. Great base for fishing trips.

Surface : **Gravel**
Spaces : **2**
Length : **<12**

77 Halsjøen

📍 60.8799, 12.3110

Photo: Tor Nordahl, ReiseMedia AS

Recreational area at Halsjøen. Swimming, sandy beach, picnic tables, outhouse, fire place, fishing, rowboat. Toll road NOK. 100, - for motorhomes.

Surface : **Gravel**
Spaces : **>10**
Length : **>12**

78 Budor

📍 60.9487, 11.2916

Parking in connection to the alpine resort. Plenty of room in the summer, but can be a lot of cars during weekends and hollidays in the winter.

Surface : **Gravel**
Spaces : **>20**
Length : **>12**

79 Bergesjøen

📍 60.9863, 11.7669

Photo: Frode Christensen

Parking at swimming area. A lot of traffic when the weather is nice.

Surface : **Gravel**
Spaces : **>5**
Length : **>10**

80 Svestua

📍 61.0004, 11.4154

Photo: Øyvind Holmstad

Site down towards Glomma (gravel)

Surface : **Gravel**
Spaces : **2**
Length : **<10**

81 Sjusjøen

📍 61.1156, 10.7410

Photo: Frisern

Parking area for winter sports resort.

Surface : **Gravel**
Spaces : **>20**
Length : **>12**

82 Trysilfjellet

📍 61.3093, 12.2426

Photo: Eivind Aursøy

Large gravel parking in connection to the alpine resort. Suitable for free camping in the summer, but can be a lot of cars on weekends and hollidays during the winter.

Surface : **Gravel**
Spaces : **>100**
Length : **>12**

83 Harptjernet

📍 61.3424, 11.2361

Photo: Roman Zacharij

Large area slightly past sand pits. Not far from Rv3

Surface : **Gravel**
Spaces : **5**
Length : **<12**

84 Mørsøybakken

📍 61.3782, 12.2127

Photo: Tor Nordahl, ReiseMedia AS

Great fishing spot down by the river. Outside toilet and shelter. Several secluded places on the same driveway.

Surface : **Gravel**
Spaces : **10**
Length : **<10**

85 Fulufjellet

9 61.3920, 12.7437

Parking in connection to the alpine resort. Good starting point for trips in Fulufjellet national park.

Surface : **Gravel**
Spaces : **5**
Length : **>12**

Photo: Morten Olsen Haugen

86 Meneset

9 61.5260, 8.8741

Recreational area with room for several campers and caravans. Sandy beach down to the water.

Surface : **Gravel**
Spaces : **5**
Length : **<10**

Photo: Håkan Svensson

87 Nordre Vikbutjønna

9 61.7845, 11.6679

Site is way off the road. Waste bin can be located close to the road.

Surface : **Gravel**
Spaces : **2**
Length : **<8**

Photo: Trond Hjermstad

88 Hamntjørna

9 61.8265, 10.2254

Campsite by an old gravel pit secluded from the road. Also the possibility of camping on the gravel site closer to the road.

Surface : **Gravel**
Spaces : **>5**
Length : **<10**

Photo: Silver

89 Veslehørsa

9 61.9034, 10.0992

Several secluded campsites at a large recreational area.

Surface : **Gras**
Spaces : **>5**
Length : **<10**

Photo: Cato Edvardsen

90 Tømmervika

9 61.9162, 11.8014

Boat ramp. Many people start canoeing from here. Not allowed for caravans but it's ok to park here with motorhome as long as you do not camp with chairs and tables outside.

Surface : **Gravel**
Spaces : **5**
Length : **<10**

Photo: Duffo6

91 Dalsvika

📍 61.9304, 11.9512

Photo: CH - Visitnorway.com

Idyllic exit with several sites under the pinewood . Nice view over Femunden. Toilets

Surface : **Gras**
Spaces : **>10**
Length : **<12**

92 Sandodden

📍 61.9404, 11.9396

Photo: Erik Jørgensen/visitnorway.com

Recreational area, also see Kongsodden at (61.9425, 11.9364) and Skinnarodden on (61.9546, 11.9368)

Surface : **Gras**
Spaces : **<10**
Length : **<10**

93 Kongsodden

📍 61.9425, 11.9364

Photo:Erik Jørgensen/visitnorway.com

Large recreational area with toilets.

Surface : **Gras**
Spaces : **>10**
Length : **>10**

94 Storlyuodden

📍 61.9663, 10.0177

Photo: Helge Stikbakke/Statens vegvesen

The campsite is at det end of the dirt road on the odd. Fishing in the river Atna. Also area closer to the road can be used.

Surface : **Gravel**
Spaces : **3**
Length : **<8**

95 Jutulhogget

📍 62.0077, 10.8974

Photo: Cato Edvardsen

Jutulhogget is Norway's second largest canyon. Not suitable for caravans but see car park at (61.9978, 10.8877)

Surface : **Gravel**
Spaces : **5**
Length : **<10**

96 Omulsoddin

📍 62.0678, 9.9869

Photo: dconvertini

Eldorado for Free Camping. Several opportunities along the road at (62.0670,9.9862 - 62.0681, 9.9837 to 62.0691, 9.9802 and 62.0681, 9.9788)

Surface : **Gras**
Spaces : **>10**
Length : **<10**

97 Follshaug

📍 62.1678, 10.5219

Photo: Jarkko Laine

Nice site down towards the river. Room for many cars. Fishing in the river Folla.

Surface : **Gras**
Spaces : **5**
Length : **<10**

98 Slettalykkja

📍 62.1866, 9.7473

Photo: Jarkko Laine

Great campground down toward the river.

Surface : **Gras**
Spaces : **<10**
Length : **>12**

99 Haldomoen

📍 62.2002, 10.3814

Photo: PeltonMan

Small free campsite in the woods behind the picnic area. Secluded and sheltered from the road.

Surface : **Gravel**
Spaces :
Length :

100 Nessvingen

📍 62.3596, 10.9000

Great site down towards Glåma. Paths along the river that are used for fishing. Several fishing spots in the area (62.3741, 10.9033)

Surface : **Gravel**
Spaces : **2**
Length : **<10**

101 Hodalsveien

📍 62.3863, 11.1246

Large gravel lot with toilet and trash containers. Very remote just aside the street but very quiet.

Surface : **Gravel**
Spaces : **>15**
Length : **>12**

102 Kjerringbekken

📍 62.4801, 11.2918

Photo: Tor Nordahl, ReiseMedia AS

Small piece of the old road that can be used for free camping.

Surface : **Gravel**
Spaces : **2**
Length : **>12**

(103) Røros Alpinsenter

Photo: esb73

⌖ 62.4836, 11.2355

979

Great parking in connection to the alpine resort. Suitable for free camping in the summer, may be a lot of cars in the winter.

Surface : **Gravel**
Spaces : **>20**
Length : **>12**

Free Campers

• GUIDE TO NORWAY 2019 •

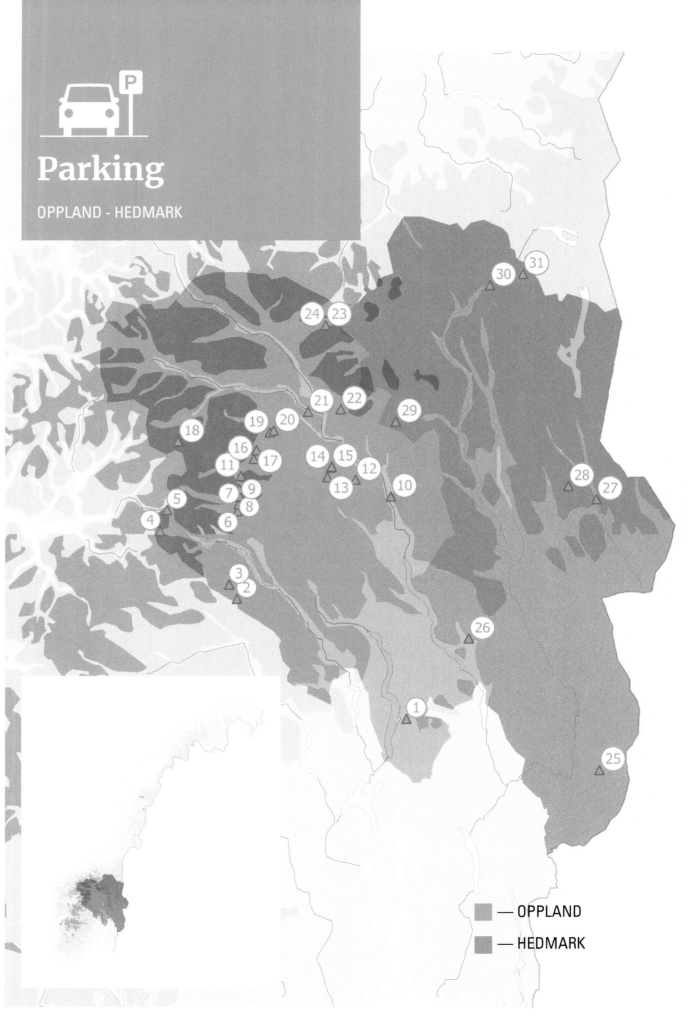

Parking

OPPLAND - HEDMARK

— OPPLAND
— HEDMARK

1 Tegneseriemuseet – Brandbu

📍 60.4171, 10.5093

143

Photo: Anders Einar Hilden

Parking at the cartoon museum. Accommodation is free for visitors to the museum. Possibility of electricity and water NOK. 50, -

Surface :	**Asphalt**
Spaces :	**>5**
Length :	**<8**

2 Flisa

📍 60.9073, 8.8807

418

Gravel parking

Surface :	**Gravel**
Spaces :	**2**
Length :	**<12**

3 Buaråne

📍 60.9690, 8.7976

424

Gravel sites on both sides of the road. Boat ramp.

Surface :	**Gravel**
Spaces :	**5**
Length :	**<10**

4 Kyrkjestølane

📍 61.1789, 8.1130

1705

Photo: Erik den yngre

Large parking lot often used by campers and caravans. Landmarks (church) and nice hiking trails in the area.

Surface :	**Gravel**
Spaces :	**>20**
Length :	**>12**

5 Tyin syd

📍 61.2777, 8.1579

1701

Photo: Tore Umes

Gravel parking with lovely views across Tyinvannet.

Surface :	**Gravel**
Spaces :	
Length :	

6 Båtskardet

📍 61.3029, 8.8093

438

Photo: Guyon Morée

Gravel parking with tables and lovely views. Starting point for hiking. Also see similar parking at 61.2998, 8.8115

Surface :	**Gravel**
Spaces :	**5**
Length :	**<12**

7 Jotunheimvegen

📍 61.3340, 8.8114

439

Photo: G.Lanting

Large gravel parking area. Amazing view.

Surface : **Gravel**
Spaces : **>20**
Length : **<12**

8 Raudesteinen

📍 61.3727, 8.8150

442

Photo:Vegar Moen

Parking. Starting point for hiking.

Surface : **Gravel**
Spaces :
Length :

9 Fisketjerni

📍 61.4041, 8.8072

445

Photo: Wener Harstad/Statens vegvesen

Parking lot, several opportunities along the road. Such as Steinplassen at 61.4026, 8.8077

Surface : **Gravel**
Spaces : **>5**
Length : **>10**

10 Fåvang kirke

📍 61.4270, 10.2190

446

Gravel site with outhouse.

Surface : **Gravel**
Spaces :
Length :

11 Vargebakken

📍 61.4645, 8.8083

449

Organized for parking - starting point for trip to Knutshø, and views to Besseggen and Gjende

Surface : **Gravel**
Spaces :
Length :

12 Nordrelia

📍 61.4916, 9.8770

454

Photo: Jan Hammershaug

Parking, also see free camp site at (61.4905, 9.8695)

Surface : **Gravel**
Spaces : **3**
Length : **<10**

13 Fagerlifjellet

61.4930, 9.6141

455

Easily accessible hikes. Not suitable for large cars. Somewhat uneven ground.

Surface : **Gravel**
Spaces : **2**
Length : **<8**

14 Feforbakken

61.5387, 9.6414

463

Photo: Jan-Tore Egge

Parking in connection with alpine resort. Plenty of space in the summer. Great area to ride a bike, go hiking, fishing etc. Toll road, bring some cash.

Surface : **Gravel**
Spaces : **5**
Length : **<10**

15 Feforkampen

61.5427, 9.6456

455

Parking lot, great starting point for hiking up Feforkampen. Relatively easy hike if you choose the route down towards the lake. Stunning views on top.

Surface : **Gravel**
Spaces : **5**
Length : **<10**

16 Besstrond

61.5473, 8.9143

467

Large parking area with a view. Kiosk.

Surface : **Gravel**
Spaces : **>10**
Length : **>12**

17 Russlivangane

61.5883, 8.9306

473

Parking lot. Starting point for hikes with bridges over Sjoa.

Surface : **Gravel**
Spaces :
Length :

18 Leirvassvegen

61.5931, 8.1930

471

Parking lot for hiking in the mountains. Leirvassbu mountain cabin at the end of the road which is the starting point for several beautiful walks on skis or on foot. Also other possibilities along the road.

Surface : **Gravel**
Spaces : **>5**
Length : **<10**

19 Turrhaugane

📍 61.6734, 9.0398

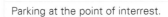

478

Photo: Kollektives Ich

Gravel site along the road. Close to Riderspranget.

Surface : **Gravel**
Spaces : **5**
Length : **>10**

20 Ridderspranget

📍 61.6838, 9.0742

478

Photo: TomasEE

Parking at the point of interrest.

Surface : **Gravel**
Spaces :
Length :

21 Veggumsvegen

📍 61.7837, 9.3799

485

You may stay overnight alongside the road.

Surface : **Gravel**
Spaces : **1**
Length : **<10**

22 Mysusæter

📍 61.8073, 9.6855

1740

Large facilitated parking lot. Often many campers here. Great starting point for hikes

Surface : **Gravel**
Spaces : **>20**
Length : **>12**

23 Avsjøen

📍 62.1823, 9.4757

131

Free parking, gravel, by Avsjøen.

Surface : **Gravel**
Spaces : **>5**
Length : **>12**

24 Avsjøen

📍 62.1823, 9.4757

501

Photo:Asgeir Helgestad/Arctic Light/visitnorway.com

Gravel parking

Surface : **Gravel**
Spaces : **5**
Length : **>10**

25 Trøsjøvegen

📍 60.2329, 12.2706

Photo: Tor Nordahl, ReiseMedia AS

Gravel parking in the cottage area near the fishing lake. Can be used if it is occupied by Fjellsjøen..

Surface : **Gravel**
Spaces : **2**
Length : **<10**

26 Martodden

📍 60.8015, 11.0261

Photo: Wassen

Large gravel site by the beach. Norwegian Jernbanemuseeum close by.

Surface : **Gravel**
Spaces : **>5**
Length : **>12**

27 Kansbekken

📍 61.4683, 12.1354

Photo: Einar Fredriksen

Part of the old road.

Surface : **Gravel**
Spaces : **1**
Length : **>12**

28 Kvannkjelda

📍 61.5216, 11.8658

Several major sites along the road.

Surface : **Gravel**
Spaces : **>10**
Length : **>12**

29 Bukjølen

📍 61.7700, 10.2120

Large gravel site with room for many cars.

Surface : **Gravel**
Spaces : **>10**
Length : **>10**

30 Bruen

📍 62.4158, 11.0182

Photo: Tore Vefferstad

Small parking in connection with the landmark.

Surface : **Gravel**
Spaces : **2**
Length : **<8**

31 Lensmannsmoen

⌖ 62.4758, 11.3298

Room for slightly larger cars or caravans. Starting point for "Nør-dalen nature- and culturepath" which is a hike in the area. Do you have a smaller camper or tent, there are opportunities for free camping in the area (62.4794, 11.3184) - (62.4794, 11.3161)

Surface : **Gravel**
Spaces : **<10**
Length : **>12**

• GUIDE TO NORWAY 2019 •

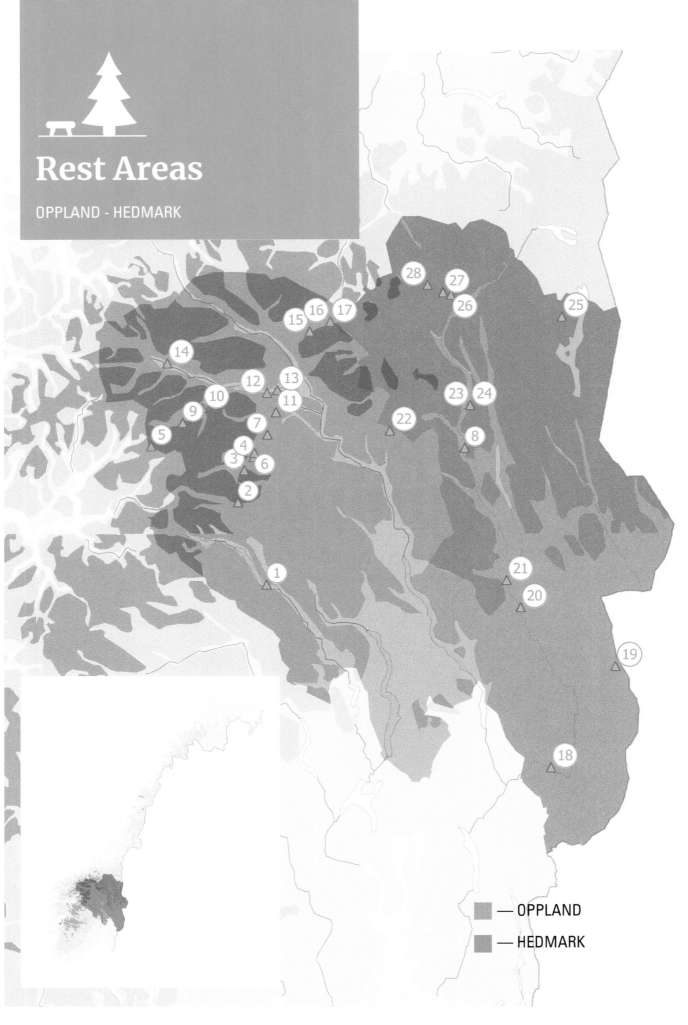

Rest Areas

OPPLAND - HEDMARK

— OPPLAND
— HEDMARK

1 Hømandbergødde

📍 60.9817, 9.1481

427

Gravel picnic area

Surface : **Gravel**
Spaces : **5**
Length : **>12**

2 Rjupa

📍 61.3427, 8.8130

441

Photo: Jarle Wæhler/Statens vegvesen

Viewpoints and picnic area.

Surface : **Beton**
Spaces : **5**
Length : **>10**

3 Maurvangen

📍 61.4914, 8.8422

453

Photo: A Froese

Picnic area down to Sjoa. Also see large parking lot at 61.4864, 8.8325 with room for over 100 cars.

Surface : **Gravel**
Spaces : **3**
Length : **<12**

4 Nedre Sjodalsvatnet

📍 61.5547, 8.9194

469

About 100m parallel to the road.

Surface : **Gravel**
Spaces : **>10**
Length : **>12**

5 Mefjell

📍 61.5587, 7.9552

470

Photo: Werner Harstad/Statens vegvesen

Large picnic area. National Tourist Route. You will also find a small site for free camping at (61.5618, 7.9549) if you want to stay somewhat off the road.

Surface : **Gravel**
Spaces : **>10**
Length : **>12**

6 Russa rasteplass

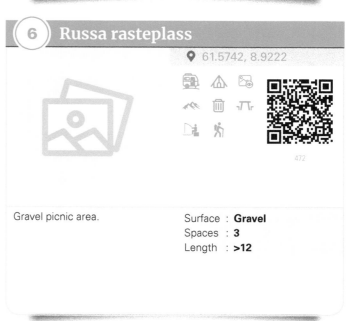

📍 61.5742, 8.9222

472

Gravel picnic area.

Surface : **Gravel**
Spaces : **3**
Length : **>12**

7 Belsen rasteplass

61.66232, 9.0276

476

Small picnic area.

Surface : **Gravel**
Spaces : **3**
Length : **>10**

8 Bjøråa

61.6684, 10.8861

Photo: Orland

You will see a large silvery elk placed at this location. This site is somewhat secluded from the road, so this site is suitable for accommodation.

Surface : **Asphalt**
Spaces : **>20**
Length : **>12**

9 Liasanden

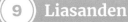

61.6796, 8.2266

479

Photo: Werner Harstad/Statens vegvesen

Idyllic picnic area in the pine woods down by the river. National Tourist road.

Surface : **Gravel**
Spaces : **5**
Length : **<10**

10 Gaupar

61.7572, 8.3950

1714

Photo: Ezzex

Picnic area and a small side road down to the river Bøvra.

Surface : **Gravel**
Spaces : **5**
Length : **>12**

11 Lemonsjøen

61.7675, 9.0874

483

Two tables. No dustbin.

Surface : **Gravel**
Spaces : **2**
Length : **<10**

12 Kvithåmåren

61.8518, 8.98801

1716

Photo: Kjenshaugmyra

Great views just off the road.

Surface : **Asphalt**
Spaces : **>5**
Length : **>12**

13 Vågåmo

📍 61.8691, 9.0808

799

Photo: Kjenshaugmyra

Large area with pier and picnic area.

Surface : **Gravel**
Spaces :
Length :

14 Heggjebottvatnet

📍 61.9405, 8.0214

1884

Photo: Hans P. Hosar

Great picnic area with beach

Surface : **Asphalt**
Spaces : **<5**
Length : **>12**

15 Steintjønne

📍 62.1453, 9.3376

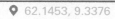

1739

Picnic area just off the road.

Surface : **Gravel**
Spaces : **>5**
Length : **>12**

16 Heglingen

📍 62.1974, 9.5268

130

Picnic area with a great view

Surface : **Asphalt**
Spaces : **>5**
Length : **>12**

17 Hegglingen

📍 62.1974, 9.5270

502

Photo: Jensens

Large picnic area just off the road

Surface : **Gravel**
Spaces : **10**
Length : **>12**

18 Sander - Rasteplasss

📍 60.2302, 11.8399

227

Photo: Tor Nordahl, ReiseMedia AS

Picnic area at the old road. Little traffic. Toilet with external water tap. Picnic tables and garbage disposal unit.

Surface : **Asphalt**
Spaces : **5**
Length : **>12**

19 Åsnes Finnskog kirke

📍 60.7036, 12.3828

Photo: Jan-Tore Egge

Parking by the beach

Surface : **Gravel**
Spaces : **<4**
Length : **>12**

20 Svingen rasteplass

📍 60.9570, 11.4896

Lot of traffic, but room for several cars.

Surface : **Gravel**
Spaces : **>10**
Length : **>12**

21 Åsta rasteplass

📍 61.0774, 11.3473

Paved picnic area with rubbish bin and table.

Surface : **Asphalt**
Spaces : **5**
Length : **>12**

22 Gututjørnet

📍 61.7252, 10.1731

Picnic area with a great view of Gututjønnet.

Surface : **Gravel**
Spaces : **8**
Length : **>10**

23 Østlund Rasteplass

📍 61.8637, 10.9120

Photo: Tor Brøndbo

Large picnic area with opportunity for secluded camping on the other side of a small lake.

Surface : **Asphalt**
Spaces : **>10**
Length : **>12**

24 Østlund rasteplass

📍 61.8641, 10.9119

Great big picnic area around a small lake. Toilets and tables. Shielded from road noise.

Surface : **Asphalt**
Spaces : **>10**
Length : **>12**

25 Tufsingdal Landhandel

📍 62.2867, 11.7353

507

Toilets, garbage bins. Canoe rental and general store. fishing spot

Surface : **Gravel**
Spaces : **5**
Length : **>10**

26 Granholtet

📍 62.3588, 10.6593

96

Photo: Hartl R

Picnic area / Free camp.

Surface : **Gravel**
Spaces : **>5**
Length : **>12**

27 Lonåsen

📍 62.3685, 10.5822

97

Picnic /gravel site by RV3 between Kvikne and Tynset

Surface : **Gravel**
Spaces :
Length :

28 Stugusjøen

📍 62.3977, 10.4300

98

Large picnic area by Fjellstugusjøen.

Surface : **Gravel**
Spaces :
Length :

111 •

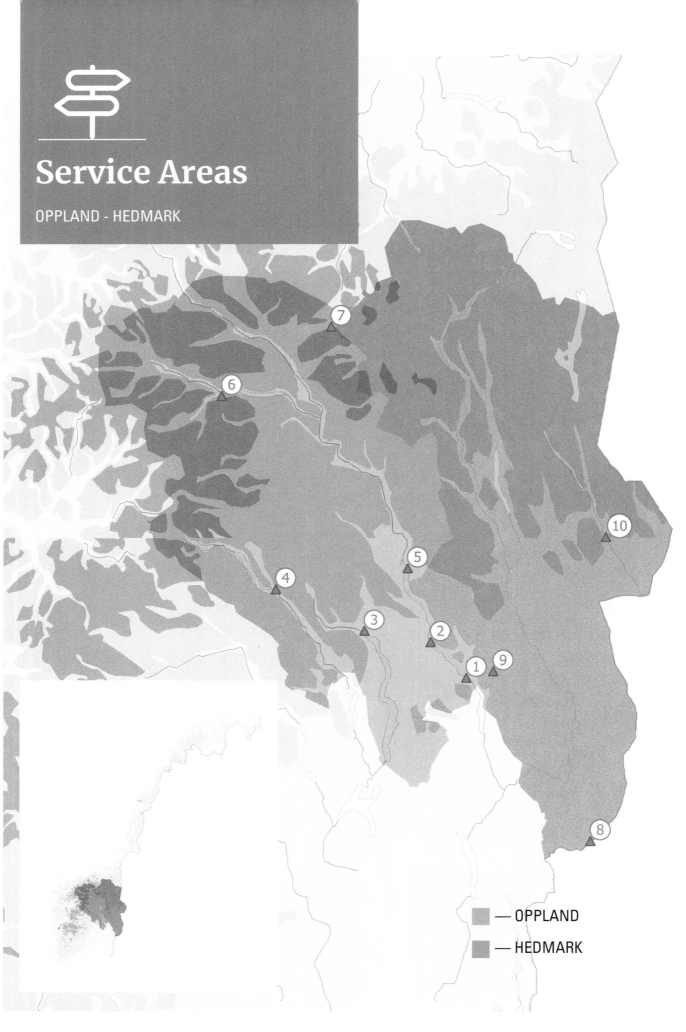

Service Areas

OPPLAND - HEDMARK

— OPPLAND

— HEDMARK

1 Totenvika
📍 60.6423, 11.0450
Upon entry at Evjua camping and Beach Park
1186

2 Gjøvik
📍 60.7953, 10.6982
Circle K, Bryggevegen 11
1179

3 Dokka
📍 60.8266, 10.0858
Wastewater treatment plant at Odnesvegen 82.
1183

4 Fagernes
📍 60.9846, 9.24391
Shell, Jernbanevegen 40
1182

5 Lillehammer
📍 61.1258, 10.4413
Lillehammer toutism center.
1180

6 Lom
📍 61.8381, 8.57028
Esso
1181

7 Hjerkinn
📍 62.1955, 9.54696
Hageseter tourist cabins.
1178

8 Morokulien
📍 59.9302, 12.2396
Morokulien picnic area.
1187

9 Hamar
📍 60.6793, 11.2862
Kolobekken picnic area E6 north
1188

10 Trysil
📍 61.3158, 12.2613
Circle K
1189

OPPLAND - HEDMARK

Rogaland

Rogaland is a county in Western Norway, bordering Hordaland, Telemark, Aust-Agder, and Vest-Agder counties. Rogaland is the center of the Norwegian petroleum industry. Rogaland is the Old Norse name of the region which was revived in modern times. The first element is the plural genitive case of rygir which is probably referring to the name of an old Germanic tribe "The Rugians". The last element is land which means "land" or "region". In Old Norse times, the region was called Rygjafylki. The largest cities are Stavanger/Sandnes, Haugesund, Bryne, Egersund, Kopervik, Ålgård/Figgjo, Kleppe/Verdalen, Åkrehamn, Kvernaland og Nærbø. Population (2017) = 473.525

Hordaland

Hordaland is a county in Norway, bordering Sogn og Fjordane, Buskerud, Telemark, and Rogaland counties. Hordaland is the third largest county after Akershus and Oslo by population. The county government is the Hordaland County Municipality which is located in Bergen. Before 1972, the city of Bergen was its own separate county apart from Hordaland. The largest cities are Bergen, Askøy, Leirvik, Osøyro, Arna, Knarrevik/Straume og Vossavangen. Population (2017) = 522.539

Sogn og Fjordane

Sogn og Fjordane is a county in western Norway, bordering Møre og Romsdal, Oppland, Buskerud, and Hordaland. The county administration is in the village of Hermansverk in Leikanger municipality. Although Sogn og Fjordane has some industry, predominantly hydroelectricity and aluminium, it is predominantly an agricultural area. Sogn og Fjordane is also home to the Urnes Stave Church and the Nærøyfjord, which are both listed by UNESCO as world heritage sites. The largest cities are Førde, Florø, Øvre Årdal, Måløy, Sogndalsfjøra og Nordfjoreid. Population (2017) = 110.230

▲ — Free Camps

▲ — Parkings

▲ — Rest Areas

▲ — Service Areas

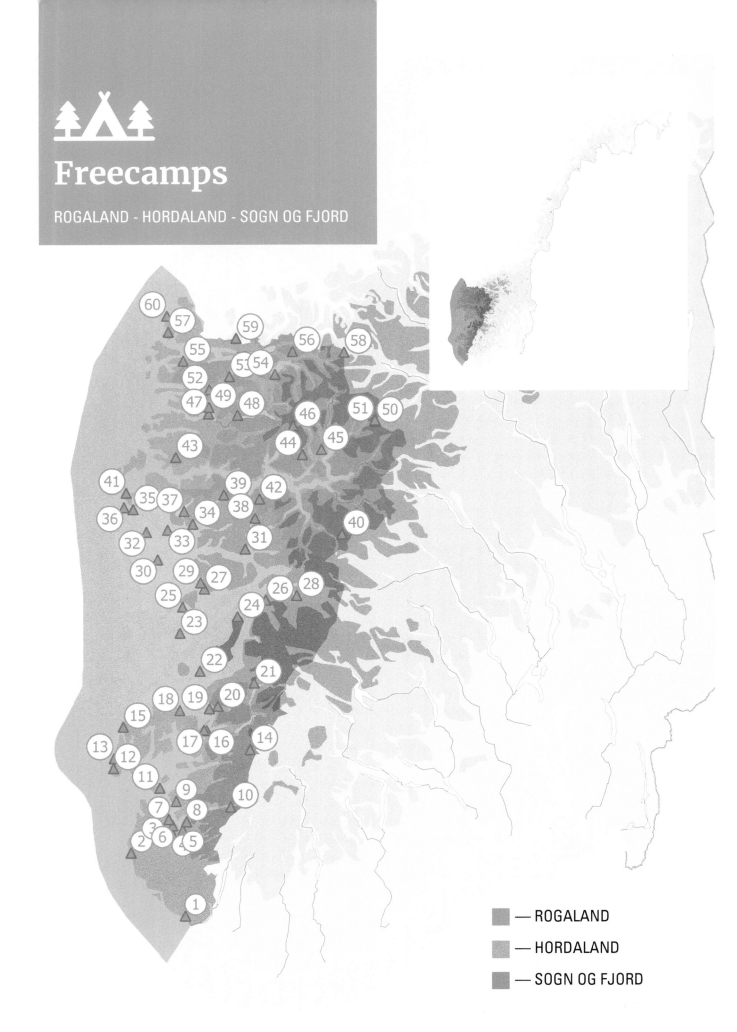

Freecamps

ROGALAND - HORDALAND - SOGN OG FJORD

— ROGALAND

— HORDALAND

— SOGN OG FJORD

1. Sogndalstrand gjestehavn

⦿ 58.3215, 6.2871

Photo: Winifred

Next to the protected buildings in Songdalsstrand. New toilet facilities and access to freshwater. No power. Free parking.

Surface : **Gravel**
Spaces : **>5**
Length : **<12**

2. Hå gamle prestegård

⦿ 58.6661, 5.5514

Photo: GAD

Parking area for visitors to the rectory. Views of the sea.

Surface : **Gravel**
Spaces : **>10**
Length : **>12**

3. Limavatnet

⦿ 58.7731, 5.9030

Photo: Usrin

Beautiful site with view overlooking Limavatnet.

Surface : **Gravel**
Spaces : **4**
Length : **>12**

4. Toberget

⦿ 58.8176, 6.0069

Photo: Rune Sattler

Large site used as rest area. Large and secluded so the site is very well suited for free camping.

Surface : **Gravel**
Spaces : **>20**
Length : **>12**

5. Oltesvik

⦿ 58.8520, 6.1213

Photo: I, Shauni

Large site (gravel) on the pier. View over Frasjorden

Surface : **Gravel**
Spaces : **>10**
Length : **<10**

6. Tengedalsvatnet

⦿ 58.8698, 5.9926

Large gravel parking lot a bit off the road, next to the swimming area at the end of Tengedalsvatnet.

Surface : **Gravel**
Spaces : **>5**
Length : **>10**

117 •

7 Eikeli badeplass / Horve

📍 58.9050, 5.9386

91

Large gravel parking in connection to the swimming area. Secluded form the road, but there can be a lot of traffic at this site on sunny days in the season.

Surface : **Gravel**
Spaces : **>10**
Length : **>12**

8 Haukalivatnet

📍 58.9054, 6.1539

87

Swimming area with accommodation. You may park in the parking lot on the other side of the road in the busy season.

Surface : **Gras**
Spaces : **5**
Length : **>10**

9 Jørpeland

📍 59.0218, 5.9966

805

Photo: rheins

Quiet gravel lot by the water, Also grassy field for tents.

Surface : **Gravel**
Spaces : **5**
Length : **<8**

10 Suleskard

📍 59.0319, 6.6529

1209

Photo: oharstad

Just off the road. The turnoff to the power station which is rarely visited. Great views down towards Kjerag and Lysebotn. Ferry Lysebotn / Stavanger. You can also check out the parking at Kjerag (59.0463, 6.6517).

Surface : **Gravel**
Spaces : **5**
Length : **<10**

11 Østhusvik

📍 59.0895, 5.7809

284

Secluded gravel site at the marina. Great views beyond Brimsefjorden.

Surface : **Gravel**
Spaces : **3**
Length : **<10**

12 Sandvesand

📍 59.1711, 5.1983

291

Photo: VisitNorway

Parking by one of Norway's finest beaches.

Surface : **Gravel**
Spaces : **<10**
Length : **<12**

13 Stavasanden

📍 59.2328, 5.1859

294

Photo: Mark Voigt

Parking by the wonderful sandy beach. Also check parking at (59.2314, 5.1771)

Surface : **Gravel**
Spaces : **>10**
Length : **<12**

14 Oddatjørns dammen

📍 59.4018, 6.7974

Photo: Martin NH

Short season - the road will not be plowed untill sometime in June. Holds a lot of cars in the area. See for example, 59.4052, 6.7970 to 59.4031, 6.7904 and 59.4136, 6.7624. Not suitable for long cars.

Surface : **Gravel**
Spaces : **>10**
Length : **<8**

15 Kvalsvik

📍 59.4353, 5.2402

321

Photo: Sergey Ashmarin

Large gravel site next to the pier, view. Swimming area nearby. Smaller cars may park along the road.

Surface : **Gravel**
Spaces : **2**
Length : **<8**

16 Sand

📍 59.4851, 6.2468

324

Photo: Cqui

Water on road to Ryfylke Museum. Sandy beach and great views

Surface : **Asphalt**
Spaces : **>10**
Length : **<10**

17 Ropeid

📍 59.4852, 6.2136

325

Photo: Reinhardheydt

An abandoned ferry pier where you may park. Separate building with toilet facilities. Great surroundings and views, almost no traffic.

Surface : **Asphalt**
Spaces : **>10**
Length : **>12**

18 Fjellstøl Skianlegg

📍 59.5889, 5.8888

935

Photo: Antje2409

Large parking at the ski resort

Surface : **Gravel**
Spaces : **>20**
Length : **>12**

19 Sauda skisenter

📍 59.6245, 6.2425

Photo: sector

Large gravel parking lot in connection to the alpine resort.

Surface : **Gravel**
Spaces : **>20**
Length : **>12**

20 Sauda Småbåthavn

📍 59.6471, 6.3406

Photo: Å MR M-Meryem

Parking at the marina. Often used for accommodation of campers.

Surface : **Gravel**
Spaces : **3**
Length : **>12**

21 Røldal skisenter

📍 59.8223, 6.7433

Photo: Mica Novotny

Large gravel parking in connection to the alpine resort. Plenty of room in the summer.

Surface : **Gravel**
Spaces : **>20**
Length : **>12**

22 Fjellhaugen Skisenter

📍 59.8531, 6.0668

Photo: arlettcsaba

Large parking areas at the alpine resort. Great for hiking in the mountains.

Surface : **Gravel**
Spaces : **>20**
Length : **>12**

23 Sundvor

📍 60.0726, 5.7584

Photo: schmimi

Large gravel site next to the road.

Surface : **Gravel**
Spaces : **5**
Length : **<12**

24 Fonna

📍 60.2268, 6.4336

Photo: Zairon

Parking in connection to the summer-ski facilities.

Surface : **Asphalt**
Spaces : **>20**
Length : **>12**

25 Eikelandsosen

⦿ 60.2411, 5.7432

Photo: Michael Breckle

Gravel site just by the waste disposal point. Great views and close to downtown.

Surface : **Gravel**
Spaces : **5**
Length : **>12**

26 Tveitafossen

⦿ 60.3521, 6.7576

Photo: A.Christensen

Parking at Tveitafossen (Tveita waterfall). Also see (60.3634, 6.7438) for slightly larger vehicles.

Surface : **Gravel**
Spaces : **<5**
Length : **<8**

27 Furedalen Alpin

⦿ 60.3723, 5.9808

Photo: meide

Large sites in connection to the alpine resort. Great base for hiking in the summer.

Surface : **Gravel**
Spaces : **>20**
Length : **>12**

28 Øvre Eidfjord

⦿ 60.4041, 7.1326

Photo: cwi.aida

Small site along the road. Also check grass area with bonfire at (60.4053, 7.1290) as well as several sites along the road.

Surface : **Gravel**
Spaces : **1**
Length : **<10**

29 Eikedalen

⦿ 60.4079, 5.9225

Photo: zibra

Parking in connection to the alpine resort. May be several cars her during weekeds and holidays in the winter. Plenty of soom in the summer.

Surface : **Gravel**
Spaces : **>20**
Length : **>12**

30 Hylkje

⦿ 60.5123, 5.3506

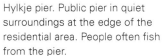

Photo: trolvag

Hylkje pier. Public pier in quiet surroundings at the edge of the residential area. People often fish from the pier.

Surface : **Gravel**
Spaces : **2**
Length : **<8**

31 Voss

📍 60.6543, 6.4187

Photo: Quevaal

Large gravel sites used for parking at the alpine resort. Plenty of room in the summer and great base for hiking.

Surface : **Gravel**
Spaces : **>20**
Length : **>12**

32 Lygra

📍 60.6744, 5.1586

Photo: Sergey Ashmarin

Lygra, just before tunnel on the left side. Gravel site for 2-3 cars without any facilities. Good fishing opportunities, quiet and calm.

Surface : **Gravel**
Spaces :
Length : **>12**

33 Kjekallen

📍 60.7072, 5.4182

Photo: Ernst Vikne

Large rest area, mainly gravel, by Kjekallen bridge. Great hiking and fishing opportunities.

Surface : **Gravel**
Spaces : **>10**
Length : **>12**

34 Mostraumen

📍 60.7655, 5.7234

Photo: Rosser1954

Spacious site (gravel) with the sea and Mostraumen just outside. Great fishingspot. Not far from Mo center.

Surface : **Gravel**
Spaces : **4**
Length : **<12**

35 Vardetangen

📍 60.8034, 4.9508

Photo: 3s

Parking at the pier

Surface : **Gravel**
Spaces : **5**
Length : **<12**

36 Langøysundet

📍 60.8063, 4.8327

Photo: Frokor

Several large sites (gravel) down towards the sea, on both sides of a quiet road.

Surface : **Gravel**
Spaces : **>10**
Length : **>12**

37 Storevatnet

📍 60.8377, 5.5894

1869

Photo: Jan-Tore Egge

Several options in the area under the bridge at the outlet of Storevatnet.

Surface : **Gravel**
Spaces : **5**
Length : **<10**

38 Myrkdalen - Voss

📍 60.8558, 6.4906

968

Photo: Nicchio

Parking in connection to the alpine resort. Plenty of room for free camping in the summer.

Surface : **Gravel**
Spaces : **>20**
Length : **>12**

39 Stølsdammen

📍 60.9746, 6.0592

423

Photo: Kim Rasmussen

There are many great sites if you drive further into Stølsheimen. The road here is a bit steep, so it is not suitable for big motorhomes.

Surface : **Gravel**
Spaces : **>10**
Length : **<8**

40 Sjurshaug

📍 60.8204, 7.6067

1925

Photo: lusentyja

Gravel site near the small lake. Great base for fishing and hikes in the mountains. Also check (60.8151, 7.6403) - (60.8112, 7.6401) and several other sites along the road.

Surface : **Gravel**
Spaces : **>10**
Length : **<10**

41 Byrknes

📍 60.8991, 4.8313

1895

Photo: Frode Inge Helland

Parking area for small boats harbor. Holds many cars. Also check Tusevågen Marina at (60.8977, 4.8436)

Surface : **Gravel**
Spaces : **>10**
Length : **>12**

42 Målsetevatnet

📍 60.9788, 6.5156

426

Photo: 2karen99

Site in front of transformer down towards the water. Also check out Ovrisvatnet at (60.9776, 6.5271).

Surface : **Gravel**
Spaces : **5**
Length : **<10**

43 Tryglevika

📍 61.1669, 5.3834

807

Small site at Espelandsvatnet. There is a small pier that can be used for swimming.

Surface : **Gravel**
Spaces : **2**
Length : **<12**

44 Sogndal – Hodlekve

📍 61.2897, 6.9841

986

Photo: Der Noks

Parking lot. Suitable for free camping in the summer. May be several cars during weekends and hollidays the winter.

Surface : **Gravel**
Spaces : **>10**
Length : **>12**

45 Sogn skisenter

📍 61.3359, 7.2193

965

Photo: sykuhe

Parking in connection to the alpine resort.

Surface : **Gravel**
Spaces : **<10**
Length : **>12**

46 Supphellebreen

📍 61.4625, 6.8212

812

Photo: Per Olav Bøyum

Parking at the foot of the Supphelle glacier. Tourist during daytime, but totally quiet in the evening and night.

Surface : **Gravel**
Spaces :
Length :

47 Storevassheia

📍 61.4666, 5.7190

1899

Photo: Jan-Tore Egge

Large sites on both sides of the road. Steep terrain so you will need bricks to get the car in level.

Surface : **Gravel**
Spaces : **>10**
Length : **>12**

48 Jølster Skisenter

📍 61.4825, 6.0920

958

Photo: zbylon

Large gravel parking lot at the alpine resort. Great for free camping in the summer,there can be a lot of cars here on weekends and hollidays during the winter.

Surface :
Spaces : **10**
Length : **>12**

49 Naustdal

📍 61.5070, 5.7137

Photo: Helge Høifødt

Great site at the Marina. Also see parking at (61.5067, 5.7181).

Surface : **Gravel**
Spaces : **>50**
Length : **>12**

50 Hervabui

📍 61.5485, 7.8742

Photo: Gerben Jacobs

Great area down towards Øvre Hervatnet, with nice view over Jotunheimen.

Surface : **Gras**
Spaces : **5**
Length : **>12**

51 Harahola

📍 61.5562, 7.8614

Photo: BIL

Nice view. Several sites along the road. Not suitable for motorhomes or big cars, but brilliant for tents.

Surface : **Gravel**
Spaces : **>5**
Length : **<8**

52 Emhjellevatnet

📍 61.6168, 5.6860

Photo: Jon Olav Eikenes

Large gravel site well off the road. Dams.

Surface : **Gravel**
Spaces : **>5**
Length : **>12**

53 Ommedalsvatnet

📍 61.7143, 5.9193

Photo: sunrayshadow

Parking down by the water at the sand pits. Possible noise from the sand pit during the day.

Surface : **Gravel**
Spaces : **5**
Length : **>12**

54 Utvikfjellet

📍 61.7659, 6.5037

Photo: Simo Räsänen

Large parking lot at the alpine resort.

Surface : **Gravel**
Spaces : **>20**
Length : **>12**

55 Svelgen

📍 61.7699, 5.2944

Photo: Stryn

Recreational area at the marina. Nice view.

Surface : **Asphalt**
Spaces : **<10**
Length : **>12**

56 Stryn vinterski

📍 61.9219, 6.6901

Photo: Andreas0815

Parking in connection to the apline resort.

Surface : **Gravel**
Spaces : **>20**
Length : **>12**

57 Vågsvåg

📍 61.9352, 5.0441

Photo: Jan-Tore Egge

Parking on the breakwater.

Surface : **Asphalt**
Spaces : **<10**
Length : **<10**

58 Stryn sommerski

📍 61.9560, 7.3634

Photo: Haakon Wibe

Open for downhill skiing in the summer. More opportunities for free camping along the road.

Surface : **Gravel**
Spaces : **>20**
Length : **>12**

59 Harpefossen

📍 61.9582, 5.9349

Parking at the alpine resort. Also check parking at (61.9670, 5.9539) which is higher up in the terrain as a good starting point for hiking. Check (61.9561, 5.9284) if you want to fish in the river.

Surface : **Gravel**
Spaces : **>20**
Length : **>12**

60 Kråkenes

📍 62.0342, 4.9937

Photo: Svein-Magne Tunli - tunliweb.no

Parking/recreational area at Kråkenses lighthouse. The weater here can be VERY rough in the fall and spring. Should not be visited by motor home in winter.

Surface : **Gravel**
Spaces : **>5**
Length : **<12**

Free Campers

• GUIDE TO NORWAY 2019 •

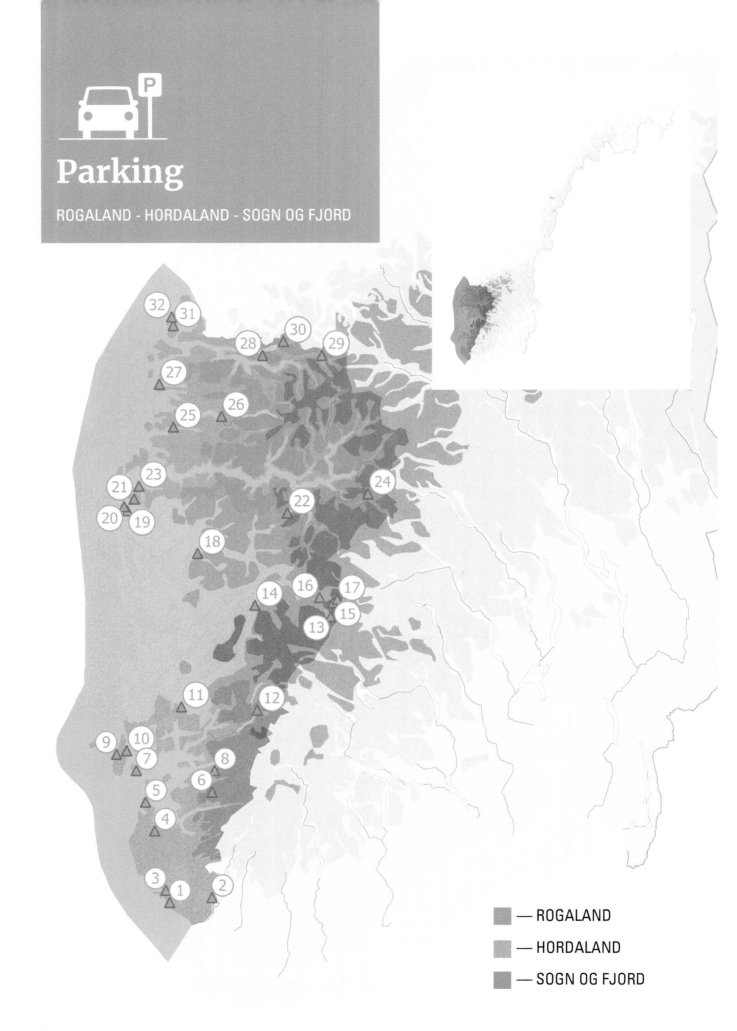

Parking

ROGALAND - HORDALAND - SOGN OG FJORD

— ROGALAND
— HORDALAND
— SOGN OG FJORD

1 Stapneshølen

📍 58.3831, 6.0666

Photo: Jarvin Jarle Vines

Parking lot, no facilities. Good fishing.

Surface : **Gravel**
Spaces : **>10**
Length : **>12**

2 Lundestranda

📍 58.4481, 6.5522

Photo: Girosch

Large parking at the museum. Also try parking / picnic area by the marina at 58.4463, 6.5532

Surface : **Gravel**
Spaces : **>10**
Length : **>12**

3 Egersund Sentrum

📍 58.4542, 6.0020

Photo: Kjetil Ree

Parking, campers accepted for accommodation. Not free.

Surface : **Asphalt**
Spaces : **>20**
Length : **<8**

4 Bråsteinvannet

📍 58.8111, 5.7752

Parking at the swimming area. BBQ facilities, soccer field and swimming area.

Surface : **Gravel**
Spaces : **>10**
Length : **>12**

5 Hålandsvatnet

📍 58.9811, 5.6183

Photo: Lene Lunde, VisitNorway

Parking lot at hiking and swimming area. Trails that go around the Hålandsvatnet. Great for fishing. Also check 58.9835, 5.6299

Surface : **Asphalt**
Spaces : **>10**
Length : **<8**

6 Sandvatnet

📍 59.1001, 6.3877

Gravel parking. Starting point for hiking and fishing in Sandvatnet or in Lyngsvatnet.

Surface : **Gravel**
Spaces : **>5**
Length : **<12**

7) Arsvågen fergekai

⦿ 59.1694, 5.4540

21

Photo: rheins

Long-term parking at the ferry dock. Room for many cars and great views.

Surface : **Gravel**
Spaces : **>10**
Length : **>12**

8) Kleivaland

⦿ 59.2359, 6.3843

Large parking lot for hiking

Surface : **Gravel**
Spaces : **>10**
Length : **<10**

296

9) Åkra

⦿ 59.2530, 5.1894

297

Photo: Mark Voigt

Large paved parking in connection with recreational area. Check also large graveled area at 59.2547, 5.1788

Surface : **Asphalt**
Spaces : **>20**
Length : **>12**

10) Kopervik, Karmøy

⦿ 59.2841, 5.3035

29

Photo: Sergey Ashmarin

Small parking lot right in the center for smaller cars.

Surface : **Gravel**
Spaces : **>5**
Length : **<8**

11) Olalivegen

⦿ 59.6033, 5.8820

1879

Photo: Ekrheim

Large parking lot for hiking or skiing in the mountains.

Surface : **Gravel**
Spaces : **>50**
Length : **>12**

12) Nesflaten kai

⦿ 59.6446, 6.8023

332

Photo: OleKj

Parking on the pier

Surface : **Gravel**
Spaces : **2**
Length : **<10**

13 Langhylen

📍 60.2870, 7.5606

379

Photo: Sergey Ashmarin

Parking lot at dam. Great fishing in Tinnhylen.

Surface : **Gravel**
Spaces : **>10**
Length : **>10**

14 Agatunet

📍 60.3021, 6.6066

380

Photo: Frode Inge Helland

Table, garbage bins, information. Parking for museum.

Surface : **Asphalt**
Spaces : **>10**
Length : **>10**

15 Skiftesjøen rasteplass

📍 60.3773, 7.5652

384

Photo: Kjersti Wold/Statens vegvesen

Gravel site just off the road.

Surface : **Gravel**
Spaces : **4**
Length : **<10**

16 Sysenvatn

📍 60.4001, 7.3919

390

Photo: NVE

Parking lot for Sysendammen. Also check graveled site at 60.4040, 7.3680

Surface : **Asphalt**
Spaces : **>10**
Length : **>12**

17 Skulevika rasteplass

📍 60.4003, 7.6148

385

Photo: Kjersti Wold

Gravel parking lot. Great starting point for hikes.

Surface : **Gravel**
Spaces : **5**
Length : **>12**

18 Dale

📍 60.5795, 5.8102

1881

Photo: Rui Simao

Parking at the sports complex

Surface : **Gravel**
Spaces : **5**
Length : **>12**

19 Bukkholmen

📍 60.7806, 4.8576

Small gravel parking / picnic area with great views.

Surface : **Gravel**
Spaces : **2**
Length : **<12**

20 Sævrøysundet

📍 60.8021, 4.8094

Small gravel parking. Awesome views

Surface : **Gravel**
Spaces : **1**
Length : **<10**

21 Gråvika gamle fergekai

📍 60.8584, 4.9191

Bjarne Thune

#VALUE!

Surface : **Gravel**
Spaces :
Length :

22 Russeviki

📍 60.9026, 6.8619

Photo: Segey Ashmarin

There are a few places along this road that can be used for smaller cars. Great views of the bay.

Surface : **Gravel**
Spaces : **4**
Length : **<8**

23 Skjerjehamn

📍 60.9417, 4.9540

Photo: Bjarne Thune

Idyllic harbor with hotels and views straight out to sea. Several sites at (60.9424, 4.9534) and (60.9407, 4.9549)

Surface : **Gravel**
Spaces : **5**
Length : **<10**

24 Borgund rasteplass

📍 61.0805, 7.8492

Paved parking. Fishing in Lærdal-selva.

Surface : **Asphalt**
Spaces : **>10**
Length : **>12**

25 Tysse

Photo: Jarkko Laine

📍 61.3422, 5.2701

1897

Parking lot.

Surface : **Gravel**
Spaces : **2**
Length : **<12**

26 Førde

Photo: Arild Nybø

📍 61.4511, 5.8624

1900

Huge parking and recreational area in the center.

Surface : **Asphalt**
Spaces : **>50**
Length : **>12**

27 Florø

Photo: Anaximander

📍 61.5952, 5.0073

1902

Parking at the pier.

Surface : **Gravel**
Spaces : **5**
Length : **<8**

28 Gautafalet

Photo: Chell Hill

📍 61.8648, 6.2812

822

Parking with great views of the fjord and glacier. Quiet and very little traffic.

Surface : **Asphalt**
Spaces : **<10**
Length : **>12**

29 Jostedalsbreen Nasjonalparksenter

📍 61.9110, 7.0471

1887

Large parking at the museum

Surface : **Gravel**
Spaces : **>10**
Length : **>12**

30 Hornindal

Photo: Ralf

📍 61.9676, 6.5265

1886

Long-term parking in the middle of Hornindal center

Surface : **Asphalt**
Spaces : **>20**
Length : **>12**

31 Kannesteinen

61.9704, 5.0691

Photo: Chell Hill

Parking by landmark.

Surface : **Gravel**
Spaces : **3**
Length : **<10**

32 Ukseneset

62.0236, 5.0309

Photo: Frokor

Parking with stunning views. Also see (62.0212, 5.0319)

Surface : **Gravel**
Spaces : **3**
Length : **>12**

Free Campers

• GUIDE TO NORWAY 2019 •

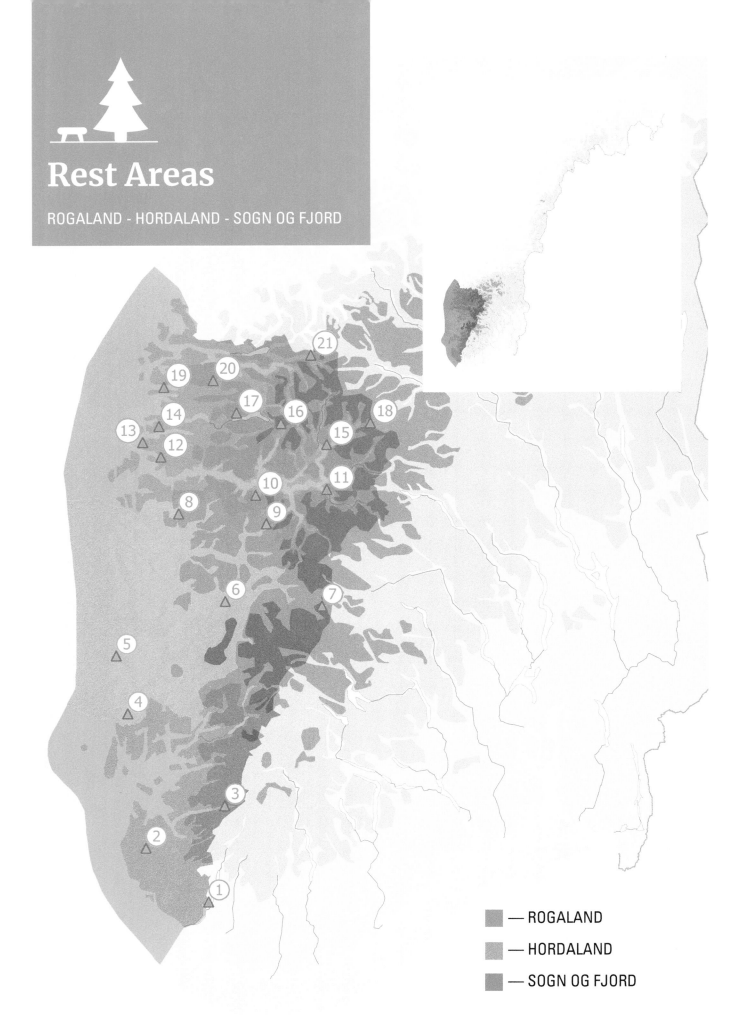

Rest Areas

ROGALAND - HORDALAND - SOGN OG FJORD

— ROGALAND
— HORDALAND
— SOGN OG FJORD

1 Tronvika

📍 58.4418, 6.6115

Large picnic area. To get to the great fishing spot, you need to walk under E39 and so, 50-60 meters along the railroad and then under the railway .

Surface : **Asphalt**
Spaces : **>10**
Length : **>12**

2 Melsvatnet

📍 58.7244, 5.7937

Photo: VisitNorway.com

Large picnic area / parking. Beautiful landscaped promenade around the water. Also check parking at 58.7241, 5.7787

Surface : **Gravel**
Spaces : **>10**
Length : **>12**

3 Lysebotn

📍 59.0497, 6.6564

Parking lot close to the waterfall, swimming. Lot of traffic at daytime in the summer season. Close to the fjords, beautiful view when it`s not raining. Also see large parking lot at (59.0458, 6.6531).

Surface : **Gravel**
Spaces : **3**
Length : **<10**

4 Hokla

📍 59.5387, 5.3482

Photo: Frokor

Picnic area with boat ramp

Surface : **Asphalt**
Spaces : **>10**
Length : **>12**

5 Kvarven

📍 59.8913, 5.1027

Photo: Margareth

Picnic area with views of the sea and Brandasund.

Surface : **Asphalt**
Spaces : **1**
Length : **<12**

6 Hereiane

📍 60.3282, 6.3380

Photo: Jeblad

Toilets and great views

Surface : **Gravel**
Spaces : **4**
Length : **<10**

7 Høgdesteinen rasteplass

📍 60.3724, 7.5417

Photo: Kjersti Wold

Large picnic area.

Surface : **Gravel**
Spaces : **>5**
Length : **>12**

8 Storevasshøgda

📍 60.8335, 5.6065

#VALUE!

Surface : **Gravel**
Spaces :
Length :

9 Stalheimsøyni

📍 60.8437, 6.7238

Picnic area with tables. Near the river

Surface : **Asphalt**
Spaces : **4**
Length : **>12**

10 Vikafjell

📍 61.0128, 6.5427

Photo: Rüdiger Stehn

Large picnic area with great views. Possibility to camp a little bit away from the picnic area, on the old road.

Surface : **Gravel**
Spaces : **>5**
Length : **>12**

11 Viki

📍 61.1035, 7.4320

Photo: Petr Smerkl, Wikipedia

Large gravel picnic area with room for several cars.

Surface : **Gravel**
Spaces : **>20**
Length : **>12**

12 Fureneset

📍 61.1713, 5.2787

Photo: Egil Husabø

Tiny picnic area. Near the road, but almost no traffic at night.

Surface : **Gravel**
Spaces : **1**
Length : **<8**

13 Laberg

📍 61.2444, 5.0203

1894

Small picnic area close to the road.

Surface : **Gravel**
Spaces : **2**
Length : **<12**

14 Holmedal

📍 61.3596, 5.1940

1898

Photo: Harald Sætre

Picnic area with great views. Also see parking at (61.3584, 5.1874)

Surface : **Gravel**
Spaces :
Length :

15 Krossviki

📍 61.3835, 7.3642

444

Photo: G.Lanting

Picnic area with benches and tables.

Surface : **Gravel**
Spaces : **2**
Length : **<10**

16 Bøyabreen

📍 61.4808, 6.7447

451

Photo: JøMa

Lovely site with a view to Bøyabreen and down to the valley. Also see parking at 61.4835, 6.7518 room for several cars.

Surface : **Asphalt**
Spaces : **>5**
Length : **>12**

17 Svidalsneset

📍 61.5108, 6.1569

458

Photo: Simo Räsänen

Large picnic area by Jølstravatnet

Surface : **Asphalt**
Spaces : **>10**
Length : **>12**

18 Silja

📍 61.5488, 7.8904

468

Photo: Werner Harstad/Statens vegvesen

Picnic area with spectacular view. Several sites for accommodation in the area.

Surface : **Asphalt**
Spaces : **3**
Length : **>12**

19 Hamrebøen

9 61.6058, 5.1825

1903

Photo: Hjorthefoto

Picnic area next to the road out towards Florø. Room for a few cars. Next to the road.

Surface : **Asphalt**
Spaces : **2**
Length : **>12**

20 Fullskjeggevatnet

9 61.6925, 5.7999

1903

Photo: sunrayshadow

Picnic area by the water.

Surface : **Asphalt**
Spaces : **<10**
Length : **>12**

21 Oppstrynsvatn rasteplass

9 61.9276, 7.0183

490

Photo: Blak-ah

Terrific view overlooking Oppstrynvatnet

Surface : **Asphalt**
Spaces : **4**
Length : **>12**

Free Campers

• GUIDE TO NORWAY 2019 •

Service Areas

ROGALAND - HORDALAND - SOGN OG FJORD

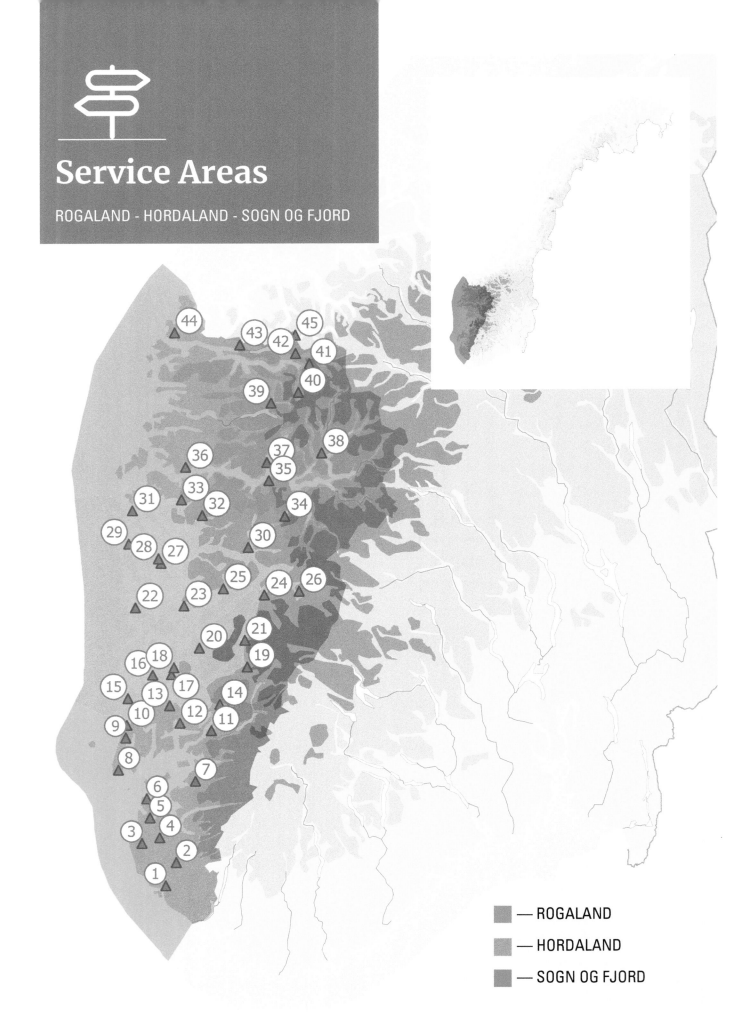

- ROGALAND
- HORDALAND
- SOGN OG FJORD

1 Steinsnes
 58.4781, 5.99649

NAF Camping - There is suposed to be free waste disposal units at site.

1145

2 Vikeså
 58.6299, 6.08207

Esso - Vikeså Veiservice, Bjerkreimsvegen 900

1144

3 Bryne
 58.7206, 5.64973

Abobil - Motorhome Dealer and motorhome parking

1155

4 Ålgård
 58.7712, 5.84793

Circle K Ålgård, Sandnesveien 40

1146

5 Stavanger – Sola
 58.8864, 5.70007

Sola motorhome AS, Vestre Svanholmen 19

1152

6 Stavanger – Randaberg
 59.0025, 5.63074

By tennis hall, Torvmyrveien 15

1151

7 Årdal
 59.1510, 6.17889

By YX gas station.

1148

8 Skudeneshavn
 59.1548, 5.24432

Shell, Vektarvegen 1

1149

9 Alvarnes
 59.3580, 5.27743

Esso

1150

10 Haugesund
 59.4371, 5.26726

Circle K Kvala, Tittelsnesveien 95

1147

11 Sand
 59.4758, 6.28900

YX Bergkrossen

1154

12 Vikedal
 59.4964, 5.89849

Vikedal marina

1157

13 Ølensvåg
 59.5974, 5.74420

Circle K

1156

14 Sauda
 59.6470, 6.34840

Osen

1153

15 Bømlo
 59.6053, 5.2325

At BEST gas station

1082

16 Vikahaugen
 59.7756, 5.48707

Parking at Circle K at Vikahaugen.

1093

143 •

17 Sæbøvik

📍 59.7941, 5.71191

Motorhome parking Sæbøvik on Halsnøy.

1088

18 Husnes

📍 59.8411, 5.72932

Waste disposal point just before the entrance to the new Halsnøytunnelen (tunnel).

1086

19 Seljestad

📍 59.9054, 6.61753

E134 towards Røldal, waste disposal point, water filling, dumpster by weight station, closed during winter.

1092

20 Rosendal

📍 59.9848, 6.0067

Skålavika.

1087

21 Odda

📍 60.0707, 6.54666

Waste disposal point at the pier just below the bus station in Odda

1091

22 Kleppholmen

📍 60.1855, 5.15284

Parking for motorhomes at Kleppholmen Marina

1094

23 Eikelandsosen Tømmestasjon

📍 60.2409, 5.7431

#VALUE!

1084

24 Kinsarvik

📍 60.3742, 6.71402

Esso gas station

1095

25 Øystese

📍 60.3815, 6.19804

Esso in Øystese

1085

26 Øvre Eidfjord

📍 60.4235, 7.13737

Måbødalen camping by RV7 in Øvre Eidfjord

1083

27 Breistein

📍 60.4855, 5.38268

At Bergen camping

1081

28 Hylkje

📍 60.5112, 5.34427

Bergen caravan and just across Bonn Gass AS

1080

29 Herdla

📍 60.5741, 4.9509

Herdla, parking lot.

1079

30 Skulestad

📍 60.6570, 6.43694

Skulestad, just behind YX gas station- open around May 1 to about November 1 (not open during winter)

1096

31 Mastrevik

📍 60.7843, 4.93139

Setenesvegen 15, bt the firehouse.

1078

32 Mo

📍 60.8171, 5.8110

Motorhome parking.

1090

33 Haugsvær
📍 60.8967, 5.51992

123 gas station by Haugsvær Auto.

1089

34 Gudvangen
📍 60.8795, 6.84360

Gudvangen, at Shell Gudvangen

1097

35 Vikøyri
📍 61.0887, 6.58570

Shell

1107

36 Lavik
📍 61.1034, 5.51224

At Circle K

1101

37 Sjøtun
📍 61.2019, 6.53141

Waste disposal units are next to Sjøtun Camping.

1098

38 Hafslo
📍 61.3024, 7.20824

Circle K, Hestnes 2

1103

39 Skei
📍 61.5759, 6.48364

Esso, free to the gas station customers.

1102

40 Briksdalen
📍 61.6646, 6.81564

Melkevoll Bretun Parking

1106

41 Lodalen
📍 61.8513, 6.91143

Sande camping

1105

42 Stryn
📍 61.9036, 6.71673

Stryn center by the taxis.

1104

43 Norfjordeid
📍 61.9120, 5.98015

At Esso

1099

44 Måløy
📍 61.9288, 5.11355

By treatment plant

1108

45 Horndøla bru
📍 62.0182, 6.68072

Horndøla bridge

1100

Møre og Romsdal

Møre og Romsdal is a county in the north western part of Norway. The county has some of Norways best known tourist attractions such as Trollstigen and the Atlantic Road. The name Møre are from a farm in Snorres saga about the king "Holy Olav" and the name Romsdal from "vally of the river Rauma". The largest cities are Ålesund, Molde, Kristiansund, Østa, Volda and Ulsteinvik. Population (2017) = 266.274

Trøndelag

Trøndelag is a county in the central part of Norway. The name Trøndelag stems from old norse for "Home of the Trøndr" and Trøndelag is one of the most fertile regions in Norway. Nidaros Cathedral and the town of Røros are attractions well worth a visit. The largest cities are Trondheim, Steinkjer, Stjørdalshalsen, Levanger og Namsos. Population (2017) = 454.596

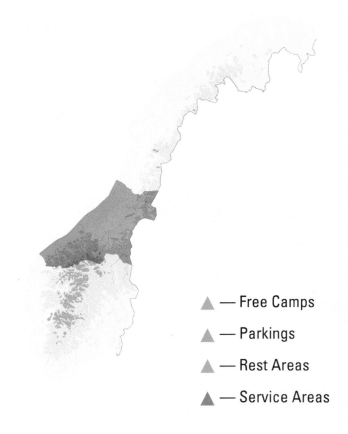

▲ — Free Camps

▲ — Parkings

▲ — Rest Areas

▲ — Service Areas

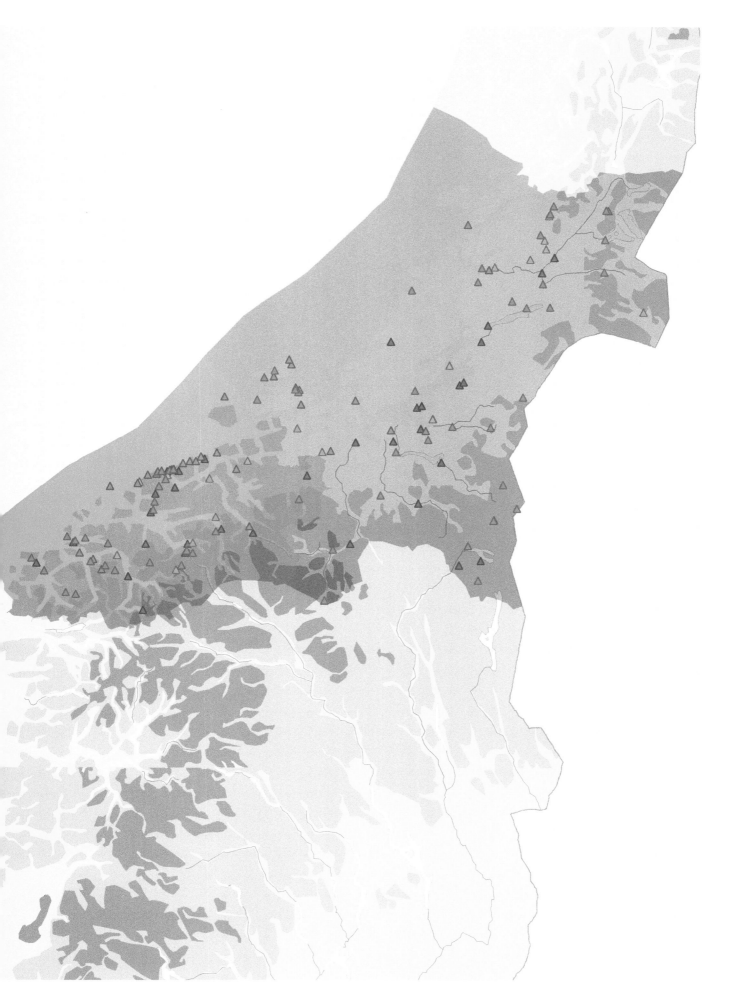

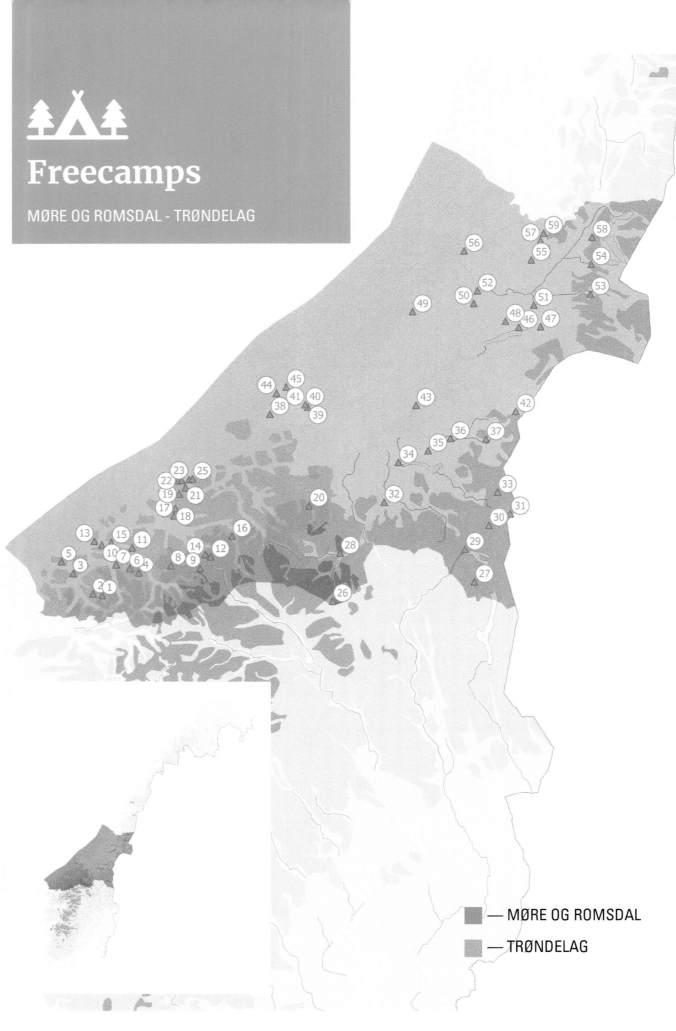

Freecamps

MØRE OG ROMSDAL - TRØNDELAG

— MØRE OG ROMSDAL
— TRØNDELAG

1 Ørsta

📍 62.1508, 6.2884

Photo: Kjetil Vaage Øie

Parking in connection to the alpine resort.

Surface : **Gravel**
Spaces : **>20**
Length : **>12**

2 Volda skisenter

📍 62.1539, 6.1524

Large parking lot that is quiet and calm out of the the ski season. Great for hiking.

Surface : **Gravel**
Spaces :
Length :

3 Kjeldsund

📍 62.2721, 5.8267

Photo: Kurth Brekke

Great place down by the gravel sitee on the pier. Canoe rental. Fishing. More possibilities in the area (62.2718, 5.8235)

Surface : **Gravel**
Spaces : **10**
Length : **>10**

4 Sunnmørsalpane Skiarena

📍 62.3354, 6.7644

Photo: Terje Sannum

Large parking lot in connection to the alpine resort.

Surface : **Gravel**
Spaces : **>20**
Length : **>12**

5 Fosnavåg Bobilparkering

📍 62.3404, 5.6339

Photo: T.Müller

This is a FREE site - with all facilities as in comercial motorhome areas. See more info on the WEB page. Free power!
Emptying the toilet and the waste water at Lanternen Marina (62.3137, 5.7082).

Surface : **Gravel**
Spaces : **>10**
Length : **>10**

6 Skålholtkrokane Sykkylven

📍 62.3573, 6.6260

Photo: Svein Skylstad

Gravel site at the fork in the road. Good walking areas.

Surface : **Gravel**
Spaces : **2**
Length : **<10**

7 Hundeidvik

📍 62.3711, 6.4248

512

Photo: Jacek Lesniowski

Gravel site and place for swimming close by. Amazing view.

Surface : **Gravel**
Spaces : **3**
Length : **<10**

8 Stordal Alpinsenter

📍 62.4117, 7.2162

989

Photo: LHV

Parking in connection to the alpine resort. Great base for hiking in summer.

Surface : **Gravel**
Spaces : **>20**
Length : **>12**

9 Longfjellelva

📍 62.4165, 7.6404

519

Photo: W. Bulach

Large gravel site. Opportunities on both sides of the road. Parking used for hikes in Reinheimen National Park.

Surface : **Gravel**
Spaces : **<10**
Length : **>10**

10 Ellingsøya

📍 62.4908, 6.1812

524

Photo: GangerRolf

Large site at the entrance to Valderøy tunnel.

Surface : **Gravel**
Spaces : **>5**
Length : **>12**

11 Grøstraumen

📍 62.5000, 6.6218

526

Photo: Frode Inge Helland

Paved exit -the old road used to go through the tunnel, but the tunnel is now closed to traffic and it is instead possible to park here. Skodjebruene on the other side of the tunnel is preserved and well worth a visit. Larger site on (62.5045, 6.6209)

Surface : **Asphalt**
Spaces : **1**
Length : **>12**

12 Romsdalshorn P

📍 62.5027, 7.7717

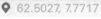

527

Photo:Snalwibma

Parking lot widely used for those who will go Romsdalshorn. Well secluded and sheltered from traffic noise. Also check (62.4979, 7.8041) with drive from Isfjorden

Surface : **Gravel**
Spaces : **10**
Length : **<12**

13 Giskebrua

📍 62.5100, 6.0645

Large grass area next to the bridge. Great beaches on both sides of the road.

Surface : **Gras**
Spaces : **>15**
Length : **>12**

14 Isterdalen

📍 62.5143, 7.6894

Photo: awiemuc

Small site by the stream. The entrance is a narrow dirt road. Not suitable for big cars or caravans.

Surface : **Gravel**
Spaces : **1**
Length : **<7**

15 Lorgja

📍 62.5164, 6.3098

Small site at the marina. Beautiful view.

Surface : **Gravel**
Spaces : **2**
Length : **<8**

16 Vistdalsheia

📍 62.6585, 8.0499

Photo: Halvard Hatlen

Big area for camping. No facilities, to stay just for the night. Good view to the mountains.

Surface : **Gravel**
Spaces : **>10**
Length : **>12**

17 Molde

📍 62.7521, 7.1702

Gravel area at the water with waterfall and dam. Also see larger parking at (62.7534, 7.1626).

Surface : **Gravel**
Spaces : **1**
Length : **<10**

18 Øyra stadion

📍 62.8038, 7.1748

Photo: Harald Groven

Lawn beside Øyra Stadium. Picnic tables and playground equipment.

Surface : **Gras**
Spaces : **>5**
Length : **>12**

19 Langvatnet

Photo: Laurent Guyot

♀ 62.9047, 7.2074

540

Great site located on a pebble beach with view over the water. Grassy area, fishing opportunities.

Surface : **Gravel**
Spaces : **5**
Length : **>10**

20 Gråsjøen

Photo: Werner

♀ 62.9178, 9.1306

1912

Recreational area at Gråsjøen. Also used as parking lot for hiking. Several opportunities in the area.

Surface : **Gravel**
Spaces : **>10**
Length : **<10**

21 Gådalsvatnet

♀ 62.9533, 7.2856

544

Starting point for a great hike to Melen. The site has room for two cars. Located at the treeline.

Surface : **Gravel**
Spaces : **2**
Length : **<10**

22 Julshamna

Nordneset Fyr

♀ 62.9952, 7.1660

550

Great little place with its own shelter, barbecue and dancefloor. The concrete pier is for camping. If you are into geocaching, there's a cache on site. The place is the starting point for StikkUt to Nordneset lighthouse.

Surface : **Gravel**
Spaces : **2**
Length : **<10**

23 Kråkholmen

Photo: Grete Kongshaug/Statens vegvesen

♀ 63.0019, 7.2177

551

Large gravel site by pier. Great views to the old trading place Teistklubben. Sculpture art on the shore. Great bike opportunities via Gjengstøa to Vevang.

Surface : **Gravel**
Spaces : **5**
Length : **<10**

24 Skarvøya

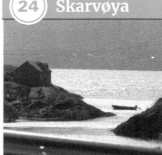

Photo: thuareck

♀ 63.0119, 7.3241

553

Gravel site at the boathouse. Amazing view. Also check (63.0122, 7.3275) on the other side of the bay. Also check out the large gravel site at (63.0108, 7.3118) where there is room for several cars.

Surface : **Gravel**
Spaces : **2**
Length : **<10**

25 Lyngholmen enkeltplasser

◉ 63.0205, 7.3730

Photo: Roger Ellingsen/Statens vegvesen

Several small exits where there is room for only one car at the time. Also check out (63.0203, 7.3715) and (63.0198, 7.3698) and (63.01097, 7.3701)

Surface : **Gravel**
Spaces : **1**
Length : **<10**

26 Svåne

◉ 62.2811, 9.5986

Photo: Juergen Haering

Just by the river Svåne. Exit with multiple parking spaces. Several opportunities in the area such as parking at (62.2791, 9.5979) and at picnic area at (62.2765, 9.5878)

Surface : **Gravel**
Spaces : **>20**
Length : **<10**

27 Rambergsjøen

◉ 62.4763, 11.6376

Photo: Jan-Tore Egge

Site on both sides of the road

Surface : **Gravel**
Spaces : **5**
Length : **<8**

28 Oppdal skisenter

◉ 62.6110, 9.6513

Photo: Sigmund Rise

Large parking in connection to the alpine resort. Excellent for free camping in the summer, but can be cramped in the winter.
Also see (62.6009, 9.6841) and (62.6152, 9.7285)

Surface : **Gravel**
Spaces : **>20**
Length : **>12**

29 Molinga

◉ 62.6940, 11.4755

Photo: Jon Østeng Hov

Great and big site by Aursunden and Molinga nature reserve. Also see (62.6922, 11.4665).

Surface : **Gras**
Spaces : **>10**
Length : **>12**

30 Mustjørna

◉ 62.8679, 11.8059

Photo:Tor Nordahl, ReiseMedia AS

There is a trail down to Mustjørna on the other side of the road.

Surface : **Gravel**
Spaces :
Length :

31 Falksjøen

⚲ 62.9529, 12.1157

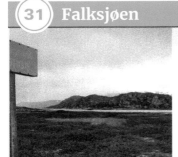

543

Large site next to dam (gravel). There are many great sites in the area. Check (62.9382, 12.1261) and (62.9291, 12.1491) just across the border to Sweden.

Surface : **Gravel**
Spaces : **>10**
Length : **<10**

32 Snøan

⚲ 62.9838, 10.2376

Photo: Jensens

Parking possibilities on both sides of the old bridge just across the river.

Surface : **Gravel**
Spaces : **>5**
Length : **<10**

33 Esandsjøen

⚲ 63.0984, 11.9098

567

Photo: Solveig Essand

Sandy beach for swimming. Also check (63.1214, 11.9148) which is a parking lot to a nice hiking area with access to toilets and water. Otherwise, many other possibilities along the road.

Surface : **Gravel**
Spaces : **>10**
Length : **<10**

34 Vassfjellet

⚲ 63.2646, 10.4042

1000

Photo: Kjetil B. Moe

Parking in connection to the alpine resort. Excellent for free camping in the summer.

Surface : **Gravel**
Spaces : **>20**
Length : **>12**

35 Nævra

⚲ 63.3571, 10.8379

573

Photo: Wikimedia Commons

Recreational area down towards the river. Holds many campers and caravans.

Surface : **Gravel**
Spaces : **>10**
Length : **>10**

36 Hegra festning

⚲ 63.4504, 11.1625

577

Photo: Cato Edvardsen

Large parking lot at the old fortifications. (museum)

Surface : **Gravel**
Spaces : **>10**
Length : **>10**

37) Meråker

📍 63.4583, 11.6964

Photo: Per Hembre

Gravel parking in connection to the alpine resort.

Surface : **Gravel**
Spaces : **10**
Length : **>12**

38) Sandvassmyra

📍 63.5197, 8.4160

Photo: Adrion

Bumpy road. Also see Brennsetra gravel parking lot at (63.5121, 8.4105). Several beautiful beaches further into Sagvatnet.

Surface : **Gravel**
Spaces : **2**
Length : **<8**

39) Oldervika

📍 63.5932, 8.9783

Fillan, Photo: Gams

Large gravel parking lot at the marina.

Surface : **Gravel**
Spaces : **>10**
Length : **>12**

40) Eidsvatnet Hitra

📍 63.6085, 8.9323

Large gravel parking right by the nice swimming area with volleyball court

Surface : **Gravel**
Spaces : **>5**
Length : **>10**

41) Eidsvatnet

📍 63.6085, 8.9323

Photo: skrisht

Swimming area with possibility for playing beach volleyball.

Surface : **Gravel**
Spaces : **<5**
Length : **>12**

42) Brudesløret

📍 63.6606, 12.1277

Photo: John Erling Blad

Lovely place down by the river. A small waterfall close by. (63.6609, 12.1241)

Surface : **Gravel**
Spaces : **5**
Length : **<9**

43 Grandfjæra friområde

◉ 63.6637, 10.6088

588

Photo: Christian Nesset

Recreational area with large parking. Swimming.

Surface : **Gravel**
Spaces : **>10**
Length : **>10**

44 Aunvågen

◉ 63.6669, 8.4811

589

Photo: Sigurd Gartmann

Gravel site at large tuurning point

Surface : **Gravel**
Spaces : **1**
Length : **<10**

45 Aunvatnet

◉ 63.7170, 8.6172

591

Photo: Jan-Tore Egge

Gravel site secluded from the road by Aunvatnet. Check also gravel site at the pier at (63.7246, 8.6182)

Surface : **Gravel**
Spaces : **5**
Length : **<10**

46 Heimsjøen

◉ 64.2337, 12.1155

614

Photo: Alasdair McLellan

Old gravel road right off the E6. The path is a bit rocky and muddy at places, so check the road before entering in wet conditions.

Surface : **Gras**
Spaces : **2**
Length : **<8**

47 Mossela

◉ 64.2439, 12.4535

114

Photo: Alasdair McLellan

Parking at the swimming area. Picnic tables and bins.

Surface : **Gravel**
Spaces : **2**
Length : **>10**

48 Bangsjøen

◉ 64.2716, 11.9044

597

Photo: Bjoertvedt

Popular area for recreation. Several possibilities in the area. Also check (64.2661, 11.8972) and (64.2762, 11.9013).

Surface : **Gravel**
Spaces : **>10**
Length : **<10**

49 Straumholet

📍 64.3007, 10.4564

596

Photo: A river near Osen.

Great recreational area with good fishing and swimming opportunities.

Surface : **Gras**
Spaces : **>10**
Length : **>12**

50 Kalvøya

📍 64.3820, 11.3964

598

Photo: Commons

Recreational area with room for many cars/wagons.

Surface : **Gravel**
Spaces : **>10**
Length : **>10**

51 Bjørgan Skianlegg

📍 64.3903, 12.3330

945

Photo: Grong Skisenter

Big parking in connection to the winter sports resort. Check also parking facilities at Grong skiresort (64.3964, 12.3189)

Surface : **Gravel**
Spaces : **>20**
Length : **>12**

52 Gullholmstranda

📍 64.4706, 11.4436

601

Recreational area just outside Namsos. Area for swimming.

Surface : **Gravel**
Spaces : **5**
Length : **<10**

53 Øystre Tverrelva

📍 64.4796, 13.2123

603

Photo: Herman Jelstad

Large parking lot for hikes to Blåfjella and Skjækerfjella. Great site for fishing in the river "Sandøla"

Surface : **Asphalt**
Spaces : **>10**
Length : **>12**

54 Litlfossen

📍 64.6852, 13.2112

609

Photo: Ketil3

Grass site out on the odd. Great fishing spot. Also check out (64.6903, 13.2160).

Surface : **Gras**
Spaces : **1**
Length : **<10**

55 Teintjønna

64.7002, 12.2649

610

Great site with views overlooking Teintjønna.

Surface : **Gravel**
Spaces : **5**
Length : **>10**

56 Abelvær

64.7392, 11.1985

611

Photo:GoogleMaps

More opportunities in the area, see also swimming at (64.7377, 11.2067) and pier at (64.7345, 11.1904).

Surface : **Gravel**
Spaces :
Length :

57 Krokneset

64.8362, 12.3974

613

Photo: suzu

Recreational area down towards the river.

Surface : **Gravel**
Spaces : **3**
Length : **<10**

58 Steinfjellveien

64.8711, 13.2130

1866

Photo: Kjartan Trana

Large gravel area. Well sheltred sites inward from this area. See also (64.8593, 13.2611)

Surface : **Gravel**
Spaces : **>20**
Length : **>12**

59 Kongsmoen

64.8871, 12.4413

616

Recreational area.

Surface : **Gravel**
Spaces : **>10**
Length : **<12**

60 Krutvatnet

65.6917, 14.3401

125

Great place down by the water. Several sites along the water, also check (65.6847, 14.4785)

Surface : **Gravel**
Spaces : **1**
Length : **<8**

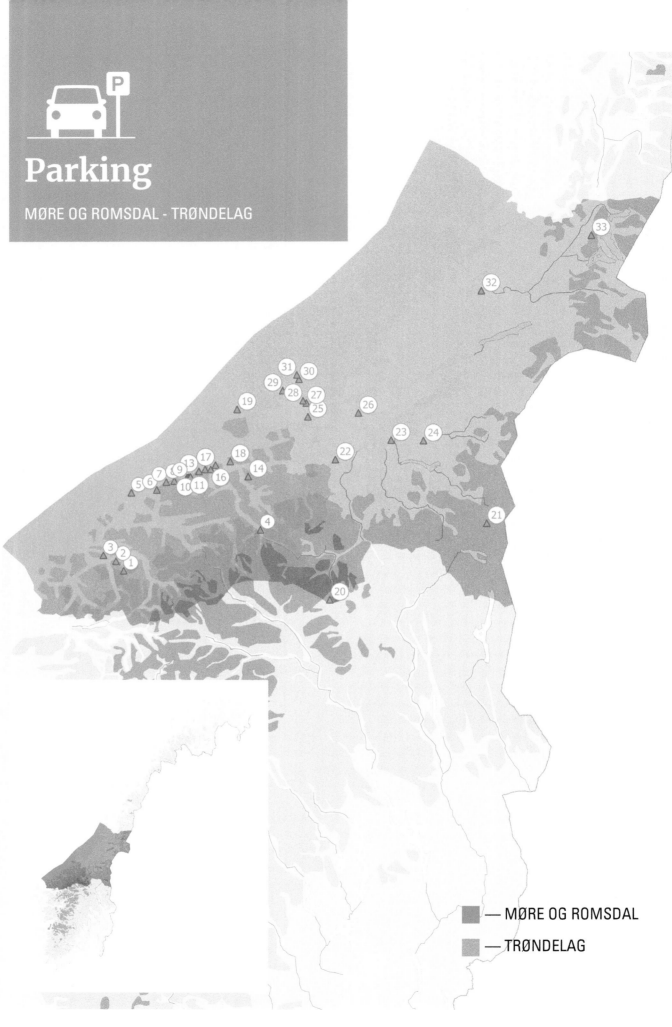

Parking

MØRE OG ROMSDAL - TRØNDELAG

— MØRE OG ROMSDAL
— TRØNDELAG

1 Straumsheims idrettsbane

📍 62.3294, 6.5842

509

Large gravel site at the sports ground. Good place for hiking!

Surface : **Gravel**
Spaces : **>10**
Length : **>10**

2 Hatlemark Sykkylven

📍 62.3870, 6.4535

515

Parking with plenty of space, gravel site. The pond near not suitable for swimming because the water sluices, good area for hiking .

Surface : **Gravel**
Spaces : **5**
Length : **>10**

3 Mausavatnet

📍 62.4162, 6.2623

Photo: Larris

1928

Parking at the water. Hike around the lake.

Surface : **Gravel**
Spaces : **5**
Length : **>12**

4 Vettamyra

📍 62.7141, 8.4930

Photo: Torlie

813

End of abandoned road. Parking for hiking trail. No facilities except a picnic table.

Surface : **Gravel**
Spaces : **2**
Length : **<10**

5 Ona – Husøy

📍 62.8652, 6.5441

536

Great site just at the ferry landing. Ona lighthouse close by, along with Ona Havstuer (cafe with hot meals and accommodation). Great sandy beach on the south side of Husøya, by the cemetery, but usually quite cold to swim.

Surface : **Asphalt**
Spaces :
Length : **>10**

6 Bud

📍 62.9066, 6.9128

Photo: Bjørn som tegner

541

Great place right behind the shop Bunnpris. Drive in Vikavegen and just to the left after about 50 meters.

Surface : **Gravel**
Spaces : **>5**
Length : **>10**

161 •

7 Askevågen

📍 62.9670, 7.0364

Photo: Werner Harstad/Statens vegvesen

Pretty site with its own lighthouse and breakwater with suitable vantage point. There is a map where islets and rocks along the horizon is marked. Near the Atlantic road.

Surface : **Gravel**
Spaces : **>5**
Length : **<10**

8 Farstadsanden

📍 62.9807, 7.1528

Photo: Grete Kongshaug/Statens vegvesen

Great base for easy hikes to the Nordneset. Beautiful beach when the weather permits.

Surface : **Gravel**
Spaces : **8**
Length : **>10**

9 Atlanterhavsvegen

📍 63.0134, 7.3303

Spectacular view and iconic site, especially on windy days. Kiosk, toilets and garbage. Space for 1-2 cars on many sites along the road.

Surface : **Asphalt**
Spaces : **5**
Length : **>12**

10 Storseisundbrua

📍 63.0169, 7.3473

Photo: Roger Ellingsen/Statens vegvesen

Many photo opportunities. Very busy road, so there is some noise. Fishing from bridges on both sides of the road.

Surface : **Asphalt**
Spaces : **>5**
Length : **>12**

11 Lyngholmen P

📍 63.0185, 7.3650

Photo: Roger Ellingsen/Statens vegvesen

Café and lookout point.

Surface : **Asphalt**
Spaces : **>15**
Length : **>12**

12 Geitøya

📍 63.0219, 7.3822

Photo: Kjetil Rolseth

Several large sites on the south side of RV64 (highway64). Fishing site with wheelchair ramp on the northeast side of the road.
100 meters to the kiosk that is selling crafts, and also to the boat to Håholmen where there is a restaurant, pub and accommoda

Surface : **Asphalt**
Spaces : **>20**
Length : **>12**

13 Langøya

📍 63.0668, 7.4944

  ⚓

560

Large open space. Views of the inner part of Reksundet and the Honningsøya.

Surface : **Gravel**
Spaces : **5**
Length : **>12**

14 Halsa fergekai

📍 63.0676, 8.2319

  ⚓

561

Great place by the sea next to the ferry dock.

Surface : **Gravel**
Spaces : **>10**
Length : **>10**

15 Vølen

📍 63.0841, 7.5835

 ⚓

562

Gravel site at the end of the road. Also parking at 63.0839, 7.5693

Surface : **Gravel**
Spaces : **3**
Length : **<10**

16 Bremsnes fergekai

📍 63.0884, 7.6671

564

Closed down ferry terminal. Large, paved area. Great views and stone sculptures nearby. Quiet area.

Surface : **Asphalt**
Spaces : **>15**
Length : **>12**

17 Vågen, Kristiansund

📍 63.1215, 7.7293

  ⚓
🗑

Photo: Harald Oppedal

566

Unregulated parking lot just north of downtown idyllic Vågen. Free. Café right next door. Dustbins.

Surface : **Gravel**
Spaces :
Length :

18 Klokkvika

📍 63.1577, 7.9433

569

Large gravel site at pier

Surface : **Gravel**
Spaces : **5**
Length : **>10**

19 Veiholmen, Smøla

📍 63.5178, 7.9588

581

Photo: Cato Edvardsen

Paved parking lot.

Surface : **Asphalt**
Spaces : **10**
Length : **<8**

20 Pilegrimsleia

📍 62.2787, 9.5973

505

Nice place with nice views. Room for several cars.

Surface : **Gravel**
Spaces : **10**
Length : **>10**

21 Langsvola, parkeringsplass

📍 62.8733, 11.8110

539

Free, not plowed in winter, gravel space, some noise form the passing cars. Several opportunities for free camping in the area, eg 62.8595, 11.8038 and Mustjørna on 62.8679, 11.8059

Surface : **Gravel**
Spaces : **>5**
Length : **>12**

22 Høgkjølen

📍 63.2394, 9.5011

572

Spacious gravel site with space on both sides of the road. No facilities

Surface : **Gravel**
Spaces :
Length :

23 Lianvatnet

📍 63.4019, 10.3126

111

Photo: Trondheim Havn

Swimming area much visited during the season. You may stay overnight off seson. BBQ / bonfire. Toilets. Also possible to park by the tram at (63.4028, 10.3137) or Lian Restaurant at (63.4029, 10.3110). Good starting point for walks in the "bymarka" forest.

Surface : **Gravel**
Spaces : **2**
Length : **<8**

24 Hommelvik

📍 63.4126, 10.7969

575

Photo: Erlend Bjørtvedt (CC-BY-SA)

Gravel site. Grass right by the sea in Hommelvik center. Sandy beach for swimming.

Surface : **Gras**
Spaces :
Length :

25 Terningsvatnet

📍 63.5164, 9.0321

Photo: Kari Raaket

Large gravel parking lot for hiking. See also exit from the road (old road) at 63.5157, 9.0299. Swimming and fishing in Terningsvatnet. During the off season you may park where the road ends at 63.5218, 9.0337

Surface : **Gravel**
Spaces : **>10**
Length : **>10**

26 Årem Småbåthavn

📍 63.5719, 9.7869

Parking at the pier.

Surface : **Gravel**
Spaces : **10**
Length : **<10**

27 Fillan

📍 63.6089, 8.9899

Parking at the pier. Also see parking at the harbor at Grisholmen 63.6081, 8.9794. And the marina with large graveled parking at 63.6021, 8.9880

Surface : **Asphalt**
Spaces : **>10**
Length : **>10**

28 Eidsvågen

📍 63.6225, 8.9364

Gravel parking at the pier.

Surface : **Gravel**
Spaces : **3**
Length : **<10**

29 Hallarelva

📍 63.6788, 8.6138

Gravel site near the road.

Surface : **Gravel**
Spaces : **1**
Length : **<10**

30 Storbåtbukta

📍 63.7666, 8.8440

Parking at the marina

Surface : **Gravel**
Spaces : **2**
Length : **>10**

31 Staulvågen

⦿ 63.7950, 8.8053

594

Nice view

Surface : **Gravel**
Spaces : **>10**
Length : **>12**

32 Spillum idrettspark

⦿ 64.4615, 11.5459

600

Large gravel parking lot in connection with sports facilities. Recreational area down towards the sea behind the site. You may also stand on Spillum pier at 64.4573, 11.5293

Surface : **Gravel**
Spaces : **>20**
Length : **>12**

33 Finnvollan

⦿ 64.8704, 13.2441

615

Parking along side the road. Several sites in the area. Starting point for hiking.

Surface : **Gravel**
Spaces : **2**
Length : **<10**

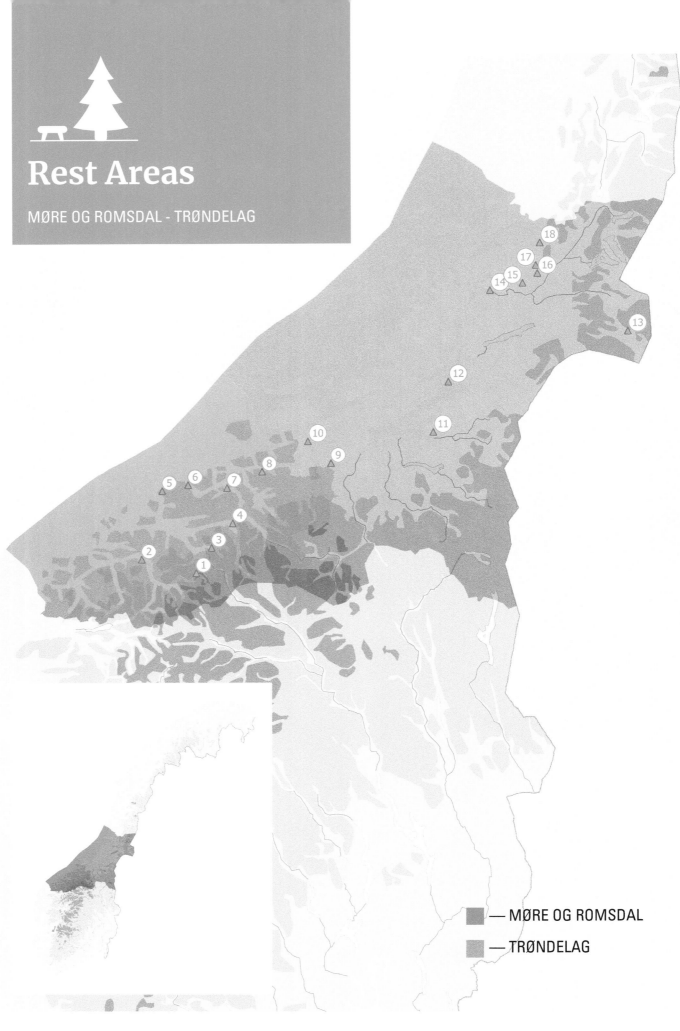

Rest Areas

MØRE OG ROMSDAL - TRØNDELAG

— MØRE OG ROMSDAL
— TRØNDELAG

1 Øvstestølen

📍 62.3843, 7.5767

514

Large picnic area. Very nice view. River flows past nearby.

Surface : **Asphalt**
Spaces : **10**
Length : **>12**

2 Ramstaddal

📍 62.4319, 6.7656

521

Small picnic area with benches and with view. Only room for 1 car.

Surface : **Gravel**
Spaces : **1**
Length : **>10**

3 Toklegjerdet

📍 62.5683, 7.7552

530

Large picnic area somewhat shielded from the road and with room for several cars. Garbage disposal.

Surface : **Gravel**
Spaces : **>20**
Length : **>12**

4 Bukta

📍 62.7520, 8.0240

533

Toilet and six large tables

Surface : **Asphalt**
Spaces : **5**
Length : **>10**

5 Fagervika

📍 62.9174, 6.9359

542

Picnic area with 2 large tables and a small path down toward the sea. Great views towards Hustadvika. Some traffic of tourists who want to stop and take pictures.

Surface : **Asphalt**
Spaces : **4**
Length : **>10**

6 Gaustadvågen

📍 62.9797, 7.3037

546

Gravel site on different levels with great views of the wetland Gaustadvågen.

Surface : **Gravel**
Spaces : **>10**
Length : **>12**

7 Bergsøysundbrua

📍 62.9895, 7.8822

549

#VALUE!

Surface : **Asphalt**
Spaces : **10**
Length : **>12**

8 Kletta bru

📍 63.1269, 8.3744

568

Large picnic area with grass areas and opportunities to park up. In walking distance to the go-cart track with fixed opening hours.

Surface : **Gravel**
Spaces : **>10**
Length : **>12**

9 Ellingsgården

📍 63.2282, 9.3867

571

Picnic area with toilet disposal point. Restaurant on site.

Surface : **Asphalt**
Spaces : **>10**
Length : **>12**

10 Nesvatnet

📍 63.3632, 9.0131

574

Picnic area with garbage disposal

Surface : **Asphalt**
Spaces :
Length :

11 Kvithammer rasteplass

📍 63.4907, 10.8824

578

Photo: Erik Fløan

Emtying grey waste and toilet. Water, table and toilet at site.

Surface : **Asphalt**
Spaces : **>10**
Length : **>12**

12 Kjerringvika

📍 63.8392, 11.0663

595

Picnic area, great place, toilet and water tap

Surface : **Asphalt**
Spaces :
Length :

13 Sandneset

📍 64.2315, 13.7946

Photo: Grong Kommune

A narrow road on the other side of the road that leads down to a small beach. May be relevant as a free camp, but park in the picnic area first then og and check if you can camp here . (64.2311, 13.7924)

Surface : **Asphalt**
Spaces : **>10**
Length : **>12**

14 Trettvika rasteplass

📍 64.4805, 11.6283

Photo: Svedenhaus

Large picnic area with secluded area for accommodation. Close to Namsos.

Surface : **Asphalt**
Spaces :
Length : **>12**

15 Hamran

📍 64.5413, 12.1335

Picnic area with information board. View.

Surface : **Asphalt**
Spaces : **4**
Length : **>10**

16 Gartlandsvegen

📍 64.6125, 12.3586

Photo: Ole Husby

Quiet and serene picnic area along Fv775

Surface : **Asphalt**
Spaces : **<10**
Length : **>12**

17 Flakkan

📍 64.6672, 12.3289

Gravel site. Fishing in Flakkan water.

Surface :
Spaces : **3**
Length : **>10**

18 Rosendal

📍 64.8226, 12.3780

2 sites in the immediate vicinity. Skogaelva goes right by.

Surface : **Gravel**
Spaces : **>5**
Length : **>12**

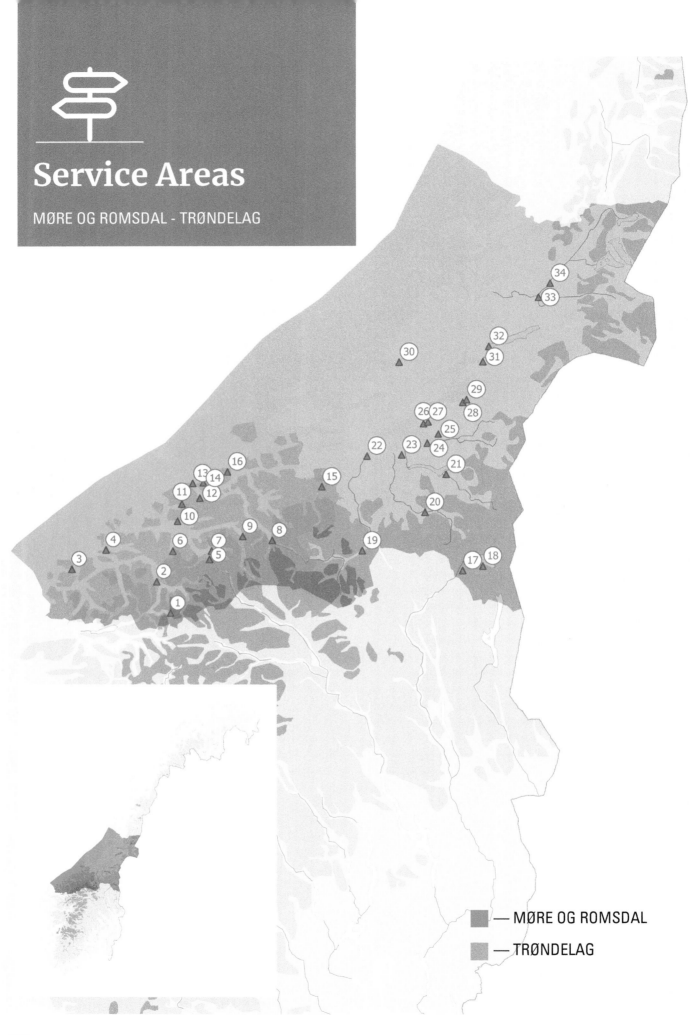

Service Areas

MØRE OG ROMSDAL - TRØNDELAG

MØRE OG ROMSDAL
TRØNDELAG

1 Geiranger
📍 62.1035, 7.2043

Wastewater treatment plant at the ferry pier

1121

2 Stranda
📍 62.3064, 6.9488

Close to Osen camping by the recycling center.

1120

3 Jensholmen
📍 62.3137, 5.7082

Lanternen marina (The lantern marina)

1113

4 Ålesund
📍 62.4766, 6.1597

Hjelsetgården motorhome parking

1125

5 Isterdalen
📍 62.4991, 7.6708

Trollstigen camping and guesthouse, picnic area with waste disposal points.

1118

6 Tresfjord
📍 62.5264, 7.1283

Best

1123

7 Valldal
📍 62.5577, 7.6868

Esso

1117

8 Sundalsøra
📍 62.6730, 8.5532

At motorhome parking

1122

9 Eresfjord
📍 62.6796, 8.1186

Coop Marked Eresfjord

1116

10 Molde
📍 62.7338, 7.1417

Close to Moldebadet and Seilet hotel.

1115

11 Elnesvågen
📍 62.8542, 7.1726

Esso

1112

12 Skjelvik
📍 62.9079, 7.4262

Best gas station

1110

13 Vevang
📍 63.0030, 7.2942

At Coop

1111

14 Kårvåg
📍 63.0150, 7.4491

At Coop Prix

1109

15 Rindal
📍 63.0708, 9.2074

YX - closed in the winter.

1119

16 Kristiansund
📍 63.1094, 7.7851

Esso Løkkemyrvegen 12

1114

17 Røros
📍 62.5657, 11.3699

At the municipal area (NPRA).

1073

18 Hitterdalen
📍 62.6034, 11.6606

Picnic area on RV31

1070

19 Fagerhaugen
📍 62.6565, 9.88127

Oppdalsporten.

1066

20 Singsås
📍 62.9493, 10.7622

Picnic area on RV30

1071

21 Selbu
📍 63.2183, 11.0420

Picnic area at Esso

1074

22 Orkanger
📍 63.3067, 9.83911

By Smart

1067

23 Heimdal
📍 63.3316, 10.3569

Sandmoen picnic area, just south of Trondheim

1075

24 Shell Stav
📍 63.4231, 10.7275

Shell gas station in both directions

1068

25 Kvithammer
📍 63.4914, 10.8839

Picnic area with service opportunity

1026

26 Hernesøra
📍 63.5568, 10.6515

Parking for motorhomes by the pier / bridge to Tautra

1018

27 Varteig
📍 63.5699, 10.7169

In the former bus station

1019

28 Gråmyra
📍 63.7179, 11.2272

South at Levanger

1023

29 Moafæra
📍 63.7381, 11.2818

Just south of Levanger camping

1022

30 Åfjord
📍 63.9647, 10.2159

YX center

1077

31 Styggmelen
📍 64.0026, 11.4982

Styggmelen 9, Løsberga

1024

32 Føllingstua
📍 64.1096, 11.5780

Camping site

1025

33 Langnes Camping
📍 64.4598, 12.3133
At the center of Grong
1020

34 Harran
📍 64.5593, 12.4852
Camping at E6 in Harran
1021

MØRE OG ROMSDAL - TRØNDELAG

Nordland

Nordland is a county in the northern part of
Norway. The county administration is in Bodø and
the remote artic island of Jan Mayen has been
administered from Nordland since 1995. The key
industries are fisheries and offshore petroleum
exploration. Turism are also important with
northern light, midnight sun and whale safaris.
There are evidence of human settlements as far
back as 10.500 years ago. The lagest cities are
Bodø, Mo i Rana, Narvik, Mosjøen and Fauske.
Population (2017) = 242.866

Troms

Troms county borders to bouth Finland and
Sweden. Due to long distance to more populated
areas, this is one of the least polluted areas of
Europe. The county administration are located
at Tromsø where also You will find the world's
northermost university, renowned for research
about the aurora borealis. The largest cities are
Tromsø, Harstad, Tromsdalen, Kvaløysletta and
Finnsnes. Population (2017) = 165.632

Finnmark

Finnmark is the northernmost and easternmost
county in Norway. The county borders to Finland
and Russia. Nordkapp are the northernmost point
of continental Europe. The name Finnmark are
from Old Norse and means "the land of the Sami
people". In Norse times the name referred to any
places where Sami people where living (also parts
of Southern Norway). The largest cities are Alta,
Hammerfest, Vadsø, Kirkenes, Bjørnevatn and
Honningsvåg. Population (2017) = 76.149

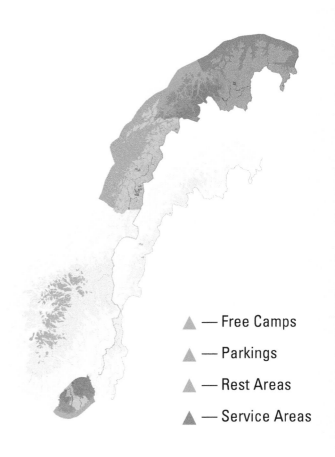

▲ — Free Camps

▲ — Parkings

▲ — Rest Areas

▲ — Service Areas

Freecamps

NORDLAND - TROMS - FINNMARK

NORDLAND

TROMS

FINNMARK

1 Semmelstraumen

📍 65.0682, 12.0404

Photo:superfredi

Site by the raod (gravel). Fishing opportunities in Semmelstraumen.

Surface : **Gravel**
Spaces : **1**
Length : **<8**

2 Bursvikbotn

📍 65.1246, 12.1623

Photo: ZWGallery

Parking on the pier at the marina. Great opportunities for fishing. You can also park at site 65.1215, 12.1704 (gravel).

Surface : **Gravel**
Spaces : **1**
Length : **<8**

3 Vennesundet

📍 65.2142, 12.0388

Photo:TorbjørnS

Recreational area just past the ferry pier. Here you can watch as the ferries come and go. Free waste disposal points at Vennesund pier next to the campsite.

Surface : **Gras**
Spaces : **10**
Length : **<10**

4 Skålvika

📍 65.3190, 12.1139

Photo: Jarle Wæhler/Statens vegvesen

Great recreational area at Vik. Beautiful view.

Surface : **Gras**
Spaces : **5**
Length : **<10**

5 Tosenvegen

📍 65.3226, 13.2795

Photo:Tor Nordahl, ReiseMedia AS

Gravel site off the road. Enclosure for labeling reindeer. Great fishing area by the river.

Surface : **Gravel**
Spaces : **2**
Length : **>10**

6 Sømnesvika

📍 65.3661, 12.1684

Photo:Jarle Wæhler/Statens vegvesen

Large gravel site with a good view. Very little traffic

Surface : **Gravel**
Spaces : **>10**
Length : **>10**

7 Rodalsstranda

📍 65.3958, 12.1712

Photo:Roger Ellingsen/Statens vegvesen

Great sandy beach with recreational area. Views to Torghatten. See also Kråkneset at (65.4361, 12.2554).

Surface : **Gras**
Spaces : **>10**
Length : **<10**

8 Kråkneset

📍 65.4361, 12.2554

Photo:Jarle Wæhler/Statens vegvesen

Recreational area at a marina

Surface : **Gravel**
Spaces : **5**
Length : **<8**

9 Urdstabbvika

📍 65.4787, 12.2747

Photo:Finnbakk

Recreational area,great for camping. More possibilities in the area. Good views.

Surface : **Gras**
Spaces : **>5**
Length : **>10**

10 Unkervatnet – Bakomsmitt

📍 65.5119, 14.1406

Photo: Silver

Large recreational area with a sandy beach. Holds many cars, great campground for spending the night in tents.

Surface : **Gravel**
Spaces : **>10**
Length : **<10**

11 Rossmålsvikja

📍 65.5877, 12.3745

Photo:Steinar Skaar/Statens vegvesen

Great area just of the road. Room for many cars / caravans.

Surface : **Gravel**
Spaces :
Length :

12 Krutvatnet

📍 65.6917, 14.3401

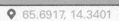

Photo: Benjamin Hell - http://www.siebengang.net/photo/

Drive all the way down to the water. Also chesk rest area at (65.6897, 14.3848).

Surface : **Gravel**
Spaces : **2**
Length : **<8**

13 Tustervasstraumen

📍 65.8023, 13.8979

Photo:Silver

Great recreational area with boat ramp. Check out the rest area within close proximity (65.8015, 13.8994) for toilets, garbage etc.

Surface : **Gravel**
Spaces : **>10**
Length : **>10**

14 Hestsundet (Tjøtta)

📍 65.8557, 12.4236

Photo:Øyvind Rask

Gravel and grass. Large recreational area next to the road. Amazing view. Several sites in the area such as (65.8581, 12.4319) and (65.8348, 12.3941).

Surface : **Gras**
Spaces : **>10**
Length : **>10**

15 Søvikvågen

📍 65.9237, 12.4313

Photo: Steinar Skaar/Statens vegvesen

Large site not far from the ferry landing. Well secluded near the marina.

Surface : **Gravel**
Spaces : **3**
Length : **<10**

16 Røssåga

📍 66.0161, 14.1167

Photo: DNT

Beautiful view and a great overnight spot if you want to explore the glacier. Narrow and steep in parts but no problem for the semi-large vehicles. Just take it slow! Several other spots along the gravel road.

Surface : **Gravel**
Spaces : **>5**
Length : **<10**

17 Leirfjorden

📍 66.0417, 12.7208

Photo:Frankemann

Site (gravel) below the bridge between Sandnessøen and Leland. Nice view. Also check out rest area at (66.0460, 12.7324)

Surface : **Gravel**
Spaces : **8**
Length : **>10**

18 Korgfjellet

📍 66.0535, 13.6958

Photo:Sandivas

Large gravel site just off the road. Accommodation is also possible at the Korgfjellet mountain lodge at (66.0544, 13.7030) and picnic area at (66.0524, 13.6826).

Surface : **Gravel**
Spaces : **>10**
Length : **>12**

19 Løkvika

📍 66.0624, 12.6754

Photo: Frankemann

Marina. Great sandy beach close by.

Surface : **Gravel**
Spaces : **2**
Length : **<10**

20 Leirfjæra

📍 66.0771, 13.0417

Photo: Jimminis

Large gravel site at the marina.

Surface : **Gravel**
Spaces : **2**
Length : **<10**

21 Storakersvatnet

📍 66.1790, 14.4819

Photo: mapio

Several nice places in this area, such as a large parking lot at (66.1819, 14.5583)

Surface : **Gravel**
Spaces : **<20**
Length : **>12**

22 Silavatnet

📍 66.3451, 13.1527

Several sites at the end of the road.

Surface : **Gravel**
Spaces : **4**
Length : **<10**

23 Storforshei

📍 66.3890, 14.5356

Photo: Sandivas

Free camp in the rest area. Sheltered from the road. Fishing and swimming in the river nearby.

Surface : **Gravel**
Spaces : **>5**
Length : **<10**

24 Vassvatnet

📍 66.3914, 13.1819

Photo: einarivers

Large site at Vassvatnet. Very little traffic.

Surface : **Gravel**
Spaces : **>10**
Length : **<10**

25 Konsvikosen

📍 66.4942, 13.0865

Photo: stefanvog

Large gravel site next to the pier.

Surface : **Gravel**
Spaces : **>5**
Length : **>10**

26 Hjaråsen

📍 66.5036, 14.9836

Photo: Pets&Paintings

Sites in the forest between the road and the river. Check also at (66.5026, 14.9838)

Surface : **Gravel**
Spaces : **>5**
Length : **>12**

27 Svesanden

📍 66.5078, 13.0302

Photo:Petter Hansen

Large site (gravel) by the sandy beach. View.

Surface : **Gravel**
Spaces : **5**
Length : **<10**

28 Jektvik

📍 66.6282, 13.2856

Photo: Daniel Vorndran

Gravel site at the marina. Not far to the ferry pier.

Surface : **Gravel**
Spaces : **2**
Length : **<10**

29 Lønselva

📍 66.6820, 15.4210

Photo: Nikolay V Aksenov

Nice free camp sites along the gravel road. There are also paved picnic area at (66.6843, 15.4177)

Surface : **Gravel**
Spaces : **>5**
Length : **<10**

30 Storglomvatnet
📍 66.7540, 14.1006

Photo: Matti Paavola

Close to the dam that Storglomvatn. Site for many capers and caravans. Several other passibilities in the area. See (66.7756, 14.1526) - (66.7700, 14.0916)

Surface : **Gravel**
Spaces : **>10**
Length : **<12**

31 Fykanvatnet

📍 66.7920, 13.9982

Photo: bReo

Great place by the water. Also check (66.7700, 14.0915) and several other places up towards the dam on Nedre Bolivatnet.

Surface : **Gravel**
Spaces : **5**
Length : **>12**

32 Storvikskaret

📍 66.9579, 13.8365

Viewpoint. There are also several opportunities along the way upwards to this site.

Surface : **Gravel**
Spaces : **2-3**
Length : **<10**

33 Storvika

📍 66.9697, 13.7864

Utsikt fra Storvikskaret

Parking at the pier. Amazing view

Surface : **Gravel**
Spaces : **3**
Length : **<10**

34 Langsanden

📍 67.1637, 14.2275

Photo: Tore Schöning Olsen

Idyllic site close to the sandy beach. Nice view. Several possibilities along the road especially if you have a slightly smaller car.

Surface : **Gras**
Spaces : **5**
Length : **<12**

35 Valnesvatnet

📍 67.1661, 14.4498

Photo: ederkoppen

Large gravel site well scluded from the road. Fishing at Valnesvatnet. Also see Vasshauet.

Surface : **Gravel**
Spaces : **<10**
Length : **<12**

36 Vasshauet

📍 67.1708, 14.4508

Photo: steffen123

Starting point for hiking. Also see Valnesvatnet.

Surface : **Gravel**
Spaces : **3**
Length : **<10**

37 Tuvlia

📍 67.2146, 14.6262

712

Parking lot for exploring sights. Stone Age settlement - among the oldest found in Norway.

Surface : **Gravel**
Spaces : **>5**
Length : **<12**

38 Heggmoen

📍 67.3550, 14.8518

714

Photo: Frankemann, Wikimedia

Site for motor home and caravan. Swimming and fishing in Vatnvatnet. Also check the parking at the dam at (67.3619, 14.8839)

Surface : **Gravel**
Spaces : **5**
Length : **<10**

39 Kobbvatn

📍 67.6313, 15.9425

836

Photo: Rob Stoeltje

Calm and beautifull lake beach with mountain view. There is a waterfall nearby.

Surface : **Gravel**
Spaces : **2**
Length : **<8**

40 Moskenes

📍 67.8955, 13.0378

715

Photo: Petr Smerkl, Wikipedia

Site (gravel). Great views and fishing. Also check (67.9016, 13.0378). For Moskenes Camping check (67.9001, 13.0529).

Surface : **Gravel**
Spaces : **3**
Length : **<10**

41 Bøsanden

📍 67.9662, 15.0527

118

Photo: mariba12

Parking at the beach. This recreational area is on the list of natural wonders in Norway

Surface : **Gravel**
Spaces : **>10**
Length : **<12**

42 Nesland

📍 68.0031, 13.2846

810

Photo: Berni245

Several exits along the quiet dirt road. Amazing views. Away from the E10.

Surface : **Gras**
Spaces : **>5**
Length : **<12**

43 Skutvik

📍 68.0137, 15.3316

718

Photo: TorbjørnS

Great site near Skutvik ferry pier. Skutvik general store and cafe just nearby.

Surface : **Gravel**
Spaces : **10**
Length : **>12**

44 Avløysinga

📍 68.0841, 13.1881

719

Photo: Mapsio

Great site at Røssøystraumen Bru. Opportunities for great fishing in the tidal currents.

Surface : **Gravel**
Spaces : **>5**
Length : **>10**

45 Hauklandstranda

📍 68.1995, 13.5297

722

Photo: DavideGorla

Claims to be the most beatiful place in Norway. Crystal clear water, white sand beach - The Arctic Paradise.

Surface : **Gravel**
Spaces : **>20**
Length : **>10**

46 Grimsøysand

📍 68.3230, 14.2022

791

Photo: Finn Rindahl

Nice small site just off the road offering a beautiful sandy beach with glorious mountain view. Great for trekking, fishing, kayaking, etc.

Surface : **Gras**
Spaces : **>5**
Length : **<12**

47 Lappstøa

📍 68.3745, 17.2532

725

Photo: Johannes Jansson

Good place for fishing

Surface : **Gravel**
Spaces : **2**
Length : **<10**

48 Laukvik

📍 68.3867, 14.4150

826

Photo: Thomas Faivre-Duboz

Several sites for you to stay in this little village. Amazing midnight sun if the weather is good!

Surface : **Asphalt**
Spaces : **>10**
Length : **>12**

49 Fiskebøl

📍 68.4162, 14.8467

Photo: Manxruler

Nice and quiet place. Use the dirt road out from the parking area through the tunnel.

Surface : **Gravel**
Spaces : **5**
Length : **<12**

50 Evenestangen

📍 68.4543, 16.7115

Photo: [illegible]

War memorial and sculpture park.

Surface : **Gravel**
Spaces : **3**
Length : **<10**

51 Vikbotnen

📍 68.6043, 14.8848

Photo: Paul Berzinn

Lovely drive to the west side of the island. Few sites for camping, but this place is gorgeous. There are other places in the area such as (68.6031, 14.8807).

Surface : **Gravel**
Spaces : **2**
Length : **<10**

52 Nyke - Tussen

📍 68.7904, 14.5198

Photo: Paul Berzinn

Site with view straight out at sea!

Surface : **Gravel**
Spaces : **5**
Length : **<10**

53 Hovden

📍 68.8114, 14.5527

Photo: Blue Elf

Great place to fish. The site is at the end of the road so very little traffic. More opportunities in the area such as (68.8163, 14.5454) and (68.7904, 14.5198).

Surface : **Gravel**
Spaces : **>10**
Length : **>12**

54 Nyksund

📍 68.9965, 15.0216

Photo: Flblbl

Several sites to stay close to the village. Beautiful view, great place to hike from.

Surface : **Gravel**
Spaces : **>10**
Length : **<12**

55 Sør-Nordmela

📍 69.1072, 15.5914

Photo: Blue Elf

Many opportunities for free camping in this area. (69.1061, 15.5885) - (69.1090, 15.5994) - (69.1127, 15.6110) - (69.1147, 15.6168). Great views over the ocean.

Surface : **Gravel**
Spaces : **>20**
Length : **>12**

56 Narvikfjellet

📍 68.4374, 17.4487

Gravel parking in connection to the alpine resort.

Surface : **Gravel**
Spaces : **5**
Length : **>12**

57 Tendringsvika

📍 68.6090, 16.5658

Photo: Ilkka T. Korhonen

No facilities. Views of Tjeldsundet. Withdrawn from the road.

Surface : **Gravel**
Spaces : **5**
Length : **<10**

58 Fauskevåg

📍 68.6711, 16.6034

Photo: Timofey Tararin

Great site for fishing and swimming, very little traffic on this road.

Surface : **Gravel**
Spaces : **5**
Length : **<10**

59 Smines

📍 68.8552, 14.9892

Photo: Blue Elf

Incredibly nice and quiet place. Beautiful views and sea fishing. Extremely low traffic as this is near the end of the road.

Surface : **Gravel**
Spaces : **5**
Length : **>12**

60 Målselv

📍 69.0726, 18.7037

Photo: Terje Lein-Mathisen

Parking in connection to the alpine resort.

Surface : **Gravel**
Spaces : **>10**
Length : **>12**

61 Sandvik

Photo: Alexander Nilssen

9 69.0859, 17.5677

753

Free camp on odd at Sandvik. Picnic area next to the facilities. Several other free camp opportunities in the area.
(69.0899, 17.5835) - (69.0899, 17.5865) - (69.0905, 17.6167).

Surface : **Gravel**
Spaces : **2**
Length : **<8**

62 Bleik

9 69.2651, 15.9133

757

Several great sites right on the dirt road that runs along the beach. Many motor homes park at Storslettneset lighthouse a little further down towards Bleik.

Surface : **Gravel**
Spaces : **>5**
Length : **<7**

63 Hatteng

9 69.2723, 19.9350

758

Large free campsite below rest area. Facilities at the rest area.

Surface : **Gravel**
Spaces : **>20**
Length : **<12**

64 Lullesletta

Photo: Marinere

9 69.3027, 20.4224

759

Parking lot used as a starting point for hiking. Large site behind the rest area for free camping.

Surface : **Gravel**
Spaces : **>10**
Length : **<12**

65 Andenes Marina

Photo: Ovuigner

9 69.3225, 16.1316

760

Gravel site at the marina. No facilities.

Surface : **Gravel**
Spaces : **10**
Length : **<12**

66 Elvevoll

Photo: Sergey Ashmarin

9 69.3521, 19.9847

817

Take the path next to the tunnel for a quiet spot out of sight. You can even follow the track to get on top of the tunnel where there is a grassy area and a campfire.

Surface : **Gravel**
Spaces : **2**
Length : **<8**

67 Skibotn

📍 69.3827, 20.2645

Photo: Matti Paavola

Free Camp on the banks of river Ivgojohka. Near the small town of Skibotn

Surface : **Gravel**
Spaces : **>10**
Length : **<12**

68 Steinfjord

📍 69.4567, 17.3477

Photo: CarmelH

Campsite down by the sea. Nice view

Surface : **Gravel**
Spaces : **>5**
Length : **>12**

69 Ersfjord

📍 69.4788, 17.3948

Magnificent views. You may park in several sites along the road or in organized parking. Hiking, swimming and fishing.

Surface : **Gras**
Spaces : **>10**
Length : **>12**

70 Senjahopen

📍 69.4963, 17.5015

Photo:Ximonic (Simo Räsänen)

Gravel site at Senjahopen

Surface : **Gravel**
Spaces : **5**
Length : **>12**

71 Laukvik

📍 69.5575, 17.6068

Photo: Göran Bengtsson

Small freecamp nearby cemetery. Great views over the sea and a sandy white beach.

Surface : **Gras**
Spaces : **4**
Length : **<10**

72 Gjellvika

📍 69.6209, 18.0652

Photo: romainprof

Grass site with stunning views over Kattfjorden. Not far from Sommarøy. The area is often used in the winter to see the northern lights.

Surface : **Gras**
Spaces : **5**
Length : **< 8**

73 Tverrbotn

⚓ 🔥 🏊

🎣

📍 69.6349, 18.4016

766

Photo: sgnd

Sandy beach with parking facilities for motorhomes and caravans. View over Nordfjorden.

Surface : **Gravel**
Spaces : **5**
Length : **<12**

74 Vågbotn

📍 69.7380, 18.4917

767

Photo: Snemann

Fantastic site with a view, close to the road but very little traffic.

Surface : **Gravel**
Spaces : **2**
Length : **<10**

75 Burfjord

📍 69.9409, 22.0466

774

Photo: Pietro Valocchi

Site with views overlooking the sea. Emptying the trash and filling of water at the gas station nearby.

Surface : **Gravel**
Spaces : **5**
Length : **>12**

76 Skogsfjordelva

📍 70.0011, 19.0780

775

Photo: supermariner

Gravel site next to the road

Surface : **Gravel**
Spaces : **7**
Length : **>12**

77 Storbekken

📍 69.7753, 30.8360

770

Photo: Dan Nordal

Large secluded gravel site next to the road. Nice view.

Surface : **Gravel**
Spaces : **>20**
Length : **>12**

78 Garajokkmoen

📍 69.8224, 23.2009

772

Picnic area with toilets.

Surface : **Asphalt**
Spaces :
Length :

79 Altaelva

 69.8317, 23.1829

Photo: Sami Keinänen

Nice site next to the river.

Surface : **Gravel**
Spaces : **4**
Length : **<10**

80 Børselvfjell

 70.3693, 25.8957

The old road to Børselvfjell. Several sites in the area such as (70.3634, 25.9305) and (70.3684, 25.8617).

Surface : **Gravel**
Spaces : **>10**
Length : **>10**

81 Vestervågen

 70.3799, 31.1187

Photo: Vardørestored

View point. Close to Vardø center

Surface : **Gravel**
Spaces : **<10**
Length : **>10**

82 Vardøya nord

 70.4044, 31.0707

Close to Vardø. Outermost on the island, by the lighthouse. Harsh area. Several sites along the way.

Surface : **Gravel**
Spaces : **>5**
Length : **<10**

83 Storsteinhøgda

 70.5942, 26.9903

Photo: Risto Varhe

Beautiful viewpoint. Holds many cars.

Surface : **Gras**
Spaces : **>10**
Length : **>12**

84 Nordkynhalvøya

 70.8019, 27.7360

Photo: Karl Brodowsky

You may park at several sites along the road - Also check (70.7981, 27.8608).

Surface : **Gravel**
Spaces : **3**
Length : **<10**

85 Slettnes fyr

⚓ 🧭 🚻 🛥

📍 71.0884, 28.2178

Photo: Torstein Johnsrud74

The world's northernmost mainland lighthouse. Toilets at the lighthouse in the opening hours.

Surface : **Gravel**
Spaces : **>7**
Length : **>12**

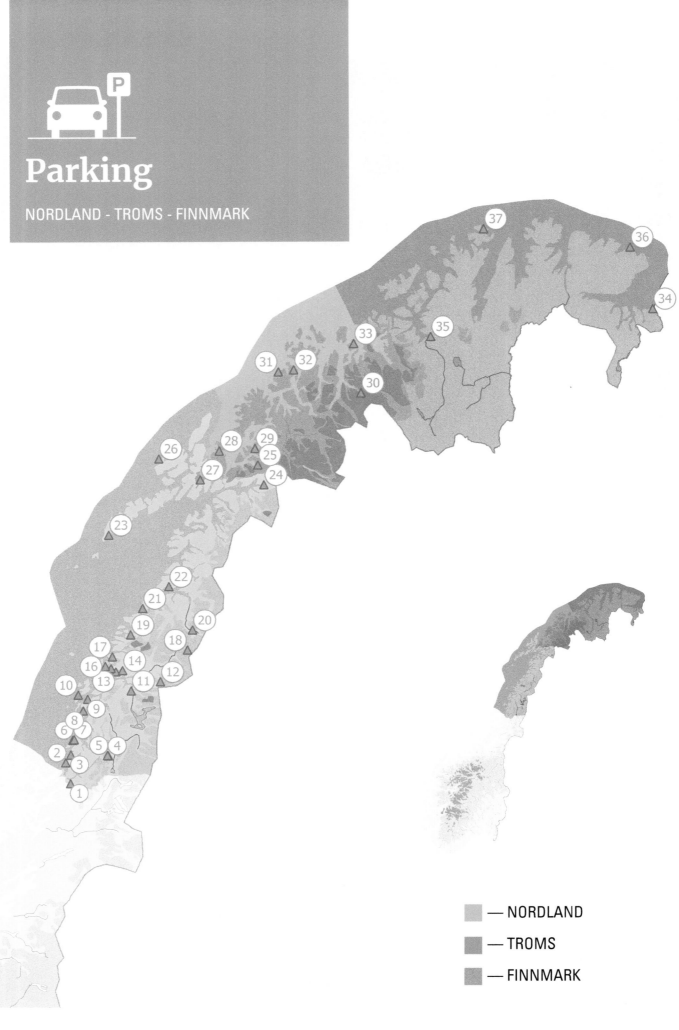

Parking

NORDLAND - TROMS - FINNMARK

— NORDLAND

— TROMS

— FINNMARK

1 Valåsen

 64.9725, 12.1682

Gravel parking next to the road. Starting point for hiking.

Surface : **Gravel**
Spaces : **5**
Length : **<10**

2 Kvennvika

 65.2109, 12.0137

Parking at recreational area with beautiful shallow sandy beach. Service building with shower and changing room. Handicap toilet.

Surface : **Gravel**
Spaces : **5**
Length : **>10**

3 Vikvågen

 65.3036, 12.1433

Parking at the marina. Great fishing opportunities.

Surface : **Gravel**
Spaces : **3**
Length : **<10**

4 Tosfjellet

 65.3097, 13.1615

Large parking lot with toilet. Base for fishing trips and tours into the national park.

Surface : **Gravel**
Spaces : **>10**
Length : **>12**

5 Tosentunellen øst

 65.3141, 13.1372

Beside the entrance to the tunnel. Large undisturbed gravel site. Also check 65.3128, 13.1400 - large gravel site on the other side of the road. And Tosenfjellet picnic area 65.3101, 13.1615

Surface : **Gravel**
Spaces : **>20**
Length : **>12**

6 Tyvika

 65.4733, 12.1764

Parking at the marina, near Brønnøysund.

Surface : **Gravel**
Spaces : **1**
Length : **<8**

7 Blomstervika, Brønnøysund

📍 65.4788, 12.2158

Photo:Mikkel Elvebakk Saidi

Free parking, close to downtown. Waste disposal points and water filling possibility close by. Below Statoil gas station. Sea fishing.

Surface : **Asphalt**
Spaces : **>10**
Length : **>10**

8 Snippen

📍 65.8194, 12.4264

Parking at the marina.

Surface : **Asphalt**
Spaces : **>10**
Length : **<10**

9 Markvoll

📍 65.9567, 12.5396

Parking for footpaths to "De syv søstre". ("The seven sisters")

Surface : **Gravel**
Spaces : **3**
Length : **<10**

10 Hestøya

📍 66.0021, 12.2690

Several possibilities in the area. Large parking area and graveled quayside.

Surface : **Gravel**
Spaces : **>10**
Length : **>12**

11 Korgfjellet

📍 66.0696, 13.7419

Large parking spot.

Surface : **Gravel**
Spaces : **>20**
Length : **>10**

12 Umskardtjønna

📍 66.1820, 14.5579

Large parking lot.

Surface : **Gravel**
Spaces : **>10**
Length : **>10**

13 Sjonfjellvatnet

📍 66.2888, 13.2998

Gravel site next to the road.

Surface : **Gravel**
Spaces :
Length :

14 Baksjøen

📍 66.3057, 13.4879

Parking at the pier.

Surface : **Asphalt**
Spaces : **3**
Length : **<10**

15 Kleiva

📍 66.3270, 13.1626

Quite and sheltered from the road. Check also great parking at 66.3281, 13.1645

Surface : **Asphalt**
Spaces : **8**
Length : **>10**

16 Grønsvik Kystfort

📍 66.3501, 13.0003

Museum and coastal forts. Several possibilities for accommodation in the vicinity. See 66.3577, 13.0063 and 66.3386, 13.0019

Surface : **Asphalt**
Spaces : **3**
Length : **<10**

17 Kvinvatnet

📍 66.4635, 13.1885

Small gravel site overlooking Kvinvatnet.

Surface : **Gravel**
Spaces : **2**
Length : **<10**

18 Polarsirkelsenteret

Photo:Manxruler

📍 66.5521, 15.3212

Parking on the Arctic Circle Center.

Surface : **Asphalt**
Spaces : **>20**
Length : **>12**

19 Skjerstøen

📍 66.7226, 13.6948

Photo: Pierre Gorissen

Parking for the ferry to Svartisen.

Surface : **Gravel**
Spaces : **>5**
Length : **<10**

20 Innervassdalen

📍 66.7828, 15.4680

Parking lot next to the road. Quite sheltered.

Surface : **Gravel**
Spaces : **5**
Length : **<10**

21 Inndyr

📍 67.0365, 14.0279

#VALUE!

Surface : **Gravel**
Spaces :
Length :

22 Vågsbotn

📍 67.2927, 14.7875

Small gravel site along the road, very little traffic.

Surface : **Gravel**
Spaces : **<2**
Length : **<10**

23 Å

📍 67.8797, 12.9774

Photo: Sam Greenhalgh

Easy to reach if you arrive from the late night ferry from Moskenes. Nice hike around a lake nearby. Can be a lot of traffic and busses in the summer season.

Surface : **Asphalt**
Spaces : **>50**
Length : **>12**

24 Langstranda

📍 68.4512, 17.7071

Large gravel site overlooking the bay and sandy beach

Surface : **Gravel**
Spaces : **>20**
Length : **>12**

25 Straumsnes

📍 68.6847, 17.5483

Gravel parking under the bridge to Årstein

Surface : **Gravel**
Spaces : **>10**
Length : **>12**

26 Nykvåg Gjestehavn

📍 68.7761, 14.4629

Photo: Blue Elf

Site for 3 cars. No facilities.

Surface : **Gravel**
Spaces : **3**
Length : **<8**

27 Gullesfjordbotn

📍 68.5294, 15.7501

Small gravel site - possibility of fishing in the river close by

Surface : **Gravel**
Spaces : **5**
Length : **<12**

28 Aunfjellet

📍 68.8613, 16.3554

Starting point for mountain walks. No facilities.

Surface : **Gravel**
Spaces : **>10**
Length : **>10**

29 Mjøsundet

📍 68.8769, 17.4821

Photo: Laturi - Wikimedia

Gravel site along side the road. Also check on the other side of the road for fricamping toward the fjord. Slompesteien picnic area is right nearby if there is no space here.

Surface : **Gravel**
Spaces : **5**
Length : **<10**

30 Kåfjorddalen

📍 69.4295, 20.9691

Starting point for several hikes and to the copper mines. Toilet. Dustbins.

Surface : **Gravel**
Spaces :
Length :

31 Gløshaugen

📍 69.7453, 18.3531

768

Parking lot.

Surface : **Gravel**
Spaces : **5**
Length : **<10**

32 Storvatnet

📍 69.7588, 18.8553

769

Large site at the end of the road.
Nice view

Surface : **Gravel**
Spaces : **>20**
Length : **>12**

33 Geitvika

📍 70.0058, 20.8975

776

Photo: Joerg Bublies

At the bridge over to Skjervøy.
Parking which is widely used for
free camping. Amazing view.

Surface : **Asphalt**
Spaces : **>10**
Length : **>12**

34 Lillesanden

📍 69.7902, 30.7934

771

Fantastic site. If you arrive some
time before noon, you will gene-
rally find a place to park , but this
place is frequently visited and
there can be many cars. Near the border to Russia.

Surface : **Gravel**
Spaces : **5**
Length : **<7**

35 Latharistranda

📍 69.9816, 23.4529

238

Photo: Uwe Durst

Parking at the recreation area.

Surface : **Asphalt**
Spaces : **>10**
Length : **>12**

36 Hamningberg

📍 70.5416, 30.6032

783

An abandoned fishing village since the 60's. Now there are only
leisure housing and old houses
here, and a summer café. Toilets
and trash cans 150m from the site.

Surface : **Gravel**
Spaces : **>20**
Length : **>12**

37 Skarsvåg

📍 71.1132, 25.8285

Photo: BishkekRocks

Large parking area. The world's northernmost fishing village!

Surface : **Asphalt**
Spaces : **>10**
Length : **>12**

Rest Areas

NORDLAND - TROMS - FINNMARK

— NORDLAND
— TROMS
— FINNMARK

1. Kollstraumen

📍 65.0399, 12.1769

Sheltered picnic area with facilities and information.

Surface : **Gravel**
Spaces :
Length :

2. Kvitnesodden

📍 65.0643, 12.0754

Gravel picnic area somewhat shielded from the road. Also see 65.0604, 12.0861

Surface : **Gravel**
Spaces : **3**
Length : **>12**

3. Hornlia

📍 65.0833, 12.0883

Large picnic area.

Surface : **Gravel**
Spaces : **5**
Length : **>12**

4. Lysfjordvatnet

📍 65.0901, 12.0839

Site close to the road. Fishing in freshwater at Lysfjordvatnet or salt water a little further out.

Surface : **Asphalt**
Spaces : **5**
Length : **>12**

5. Vikahøgda

📍 65.1213, 12.1382

Picnic area close to the road, great views.

Surface : **Asphalt**
Spaces : **5**
Length : **>12**

6. Gamle Holmsveien

📍 65.1705, 12.1151

The old road. Great views but a bit cramped and close to the road.

Surface : **Gravel**
Spaces : **2**
Length : **>10**

7 Holmsvågen / Gimlingen

📍 65.1839, 12.1172

629

Picnic area right by the ferry dock. Great views but close to the road.

Surface : **Gravel**
Spaces : **>5**
Length : **>12**

8 Tosfjellet

📍 65.3096, 13.1619

634

Large gravel picnic area with great views. Also check site by dam at 65.3109, 13.1634

Surface : **Gravel**
Spaces : **>10**
Length : **>12**

9 Krutvatnet – Rasteplass

📍 65.6898, 14.3840

126

Picnic area with picnic table and outhouse

Surface : **Asphalt**
Spaces : **>3**
Length : **>12**

10 Skreingan

📍 66.0291, 12.6969

Photo: Steinar Skaar/Statens vegvesen

659

Sculpture landscape - Picnic area. Also see free camp site at 66.0417, 12.7208

Surface : **Asphalt**
Spaces : **4**
Length : **<10**

11 Lille Luktvatnet

📍 66.0488, 13.6097

662

Large picnic area. Nice view

Surface : **Asphalt**
Spaces :
Length :

12 Sjonfjellet

📍 66.2815, 13.2611

675

Picnic area with viewpoint.

Surface : **Asphalt**
Spaces :
Length :

13 Hellåga Rasteplass

📍 66.3138, 13.2839

Photo: Steianr Skaar/Statens vegvesen

Upgraded restarea as part of the national tourist routes.

Surface : **Asphalt**
Spaces : **>5**
Length : **>12**

14 Hanna Kvanmos plass

📍 66.3193, 13.3105

Picnic area that is accessible for campers. Also possible to park / stay on the grass.

Surface : **Asphalt**
Spaces : **>10**
Length : **>10**

15 Saltfjellet

📍 66.6126, 15.3676

Large picnic area with nice views.

Surface : **Asphalt**
Spaces : **>10**
Length : **>12**

16 Reppa rasteplass

📍 66.6466, 13.5349

Great views, room for several cars

Surface : **Asphalt**
Spaces : **>10**
Length : **>10**

17 Ågvatnet

📍 66.7049, 13.4703

Table, garbage cans, bonfire

Surface : **Gravel**
Spaces : **3**
Length : **<10**

18 Holand rasteplass

📍 66.7244, 13.6982

Waste sisposal points, toilets, dustbins. Sculpture and lookout point. Information about the ferry to Svartisen. Also check Skjerstø- en at the pier for the boat to Svartisen.

Surface : **Asphalt**
Spaces : **5**
Length : **>12**

19 Reipå sør

66.8956, 13.6493

Photo: Øyvind Rask

Great parking in connection to the swimming area / sandy beach.

Surface : **Gravel**
Spaces :
Length :

700

20 Storvika rasteplass

66.9599, 13.8030

Photo: Lasse Karstensen

Waste disposal point for motorhomes.

Surface : **Asphalt**
Spaces : **>10**
Length : **>12**

702

21 Djupvatnet

67.1653, 14.4372

picnic area

Surface : **Gravel**
Spaces : **2**
Length : **<10**

707

22 Osan

67.1784, 14.5742

Fishing. Accommodates up to 5 cars. Check 67.1804, 14.5984 if there is no room here. Not far from Saltstraumen.

Surface : **Asphalt**
Spaces : **5**
Length : **>12**

710

23 Forsbukta

67.9511, 15.6330

Picnic area with separate section for motorhome parking Sculptures on site.

Surface : **Asphalt**
Spaces : **5**
Length : **>12**

716

24 Flakstad

68.1038, 13.2835

Photo: Marco Usan

Great spot to stay overnight. Stunning beach and surrounding mountains. Toilets and running water available.

Surface : **Asphalt**
Spaces : **>15**
Length : **>12**

793

(25) Hagskaret

📍 68.1581, 13.6923

720

Large picnic area with toilets, tables and garbage cans. Well sheltered from the road. There is also a gravel turnoff at (68.1555, 13.7106) which may have less traffic.

Surface : **Asphalt**
Spaces : **>20**
Length : **>12**

(26) Eggum

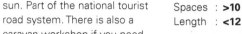
Photo: Marco Usan

📍 68.3069, 13.6508

823

Great place to see the midnight sun. Part of the national tourist road system. There is also a caravan workshop if you need services. NOK 100, - Also see possible site at (68.3054, 13.6964)

Surface : **Gravel**
Spaces : **>10**
Length : **<12**

(27) Autsnesfjorden

📍 68.3158, 14.7158

723

Table, garbage bins and lookout spot.

Surface : **Asphalt**
Spaces : **8**
Length : **>10**

(28) Forneset

📍 68.3841, 17.2538

726

Memorials of General Fleischer. Good fishing spot.

Surface : **Gravel**
Spaces : **>5**
Length : **>12**

(29) Kanstadbotn

📍 68.4999, 15.8834

731

Gravel site by the road. Some traffic.

Surface : **Gravel**
Spaces : **7**
Length : **>12**

(30) Gullesfjordbotn

📍 68.5301, 15.7617

733

Large paved sites. Weight on one side of the road.

Surface : **Asphalt**
Spaces : **>20**
Length : **>12**

31 Løbergsbukta

📍 68.5598, 15.7514

734

Picnic area just off the highway. Some traffic passes by. Nice views of the bay. Fishing in Løbergsvannet. Foothpath. Also starting point for hikes to the DNT Snytindhytta (The Norwegian Trekking Association). Garbage cans.

Surface : **Gravel**
Spaces :
Length :

32 Kviteberget

📍 68.5662, 16.6644

736

Exit with toilet at site. Plenty of room for several cars.

Surface : **Asphalt**
Spaces : **>5**
Length : **>12**

33 Sigerfjordhøgda

📍 68.6613, 15.5004

739

Photo: Blue Elf

Picnic area with great views of Sigerfjorden.

Surface : **Asphalt**
Spaces : **8**
Length : **>12**

34 Nupsviken

📍 68.8629, 16.2382

750

Picnic area, often used to see the midnight sun. Great views of Kasfjorden.

Surface : **Gravel**
Spaces :
Length :

35 Slompesteien

📍 68.8849, 17.4657

752

Photo: Laturi - Wikimedia

Picnic area with garbage disposal units, toilets and picnic tables. Lots of fish in the water, pollock. Nice view.

Surface : **Gravel**
Spaces : **>5**
Length : **>12**

36 Heia

📍 69.1422, 19.0541

755

Access for motorhomes and caravans.

Surface : **Gravel**
Spaces : **>20**
Length : **>12**

37 Galbanjarga

69.2441, 23.7919

1875

Photo: Peter Van den Bossche

Large picnic area by the water. Room for several cars and caravans.

Surface : **Asphalt**
Spaces : **10**
Length : **>12**

38 Bjørnnes rasteplass

70.1043, 24.9192

778

Plowed in winter.

Surface : **Asphalt**
Spaces : **>5**
Length : **>12**

39 Polmasjokka rasteplass – Russevatnet

70.4179, 25.1518

782

Tables and toilets.

Surface : **Asphalt**
Spaces : **5**
Length : **>12**

Service Areas

NORDLAND - TROMS - FINNMARK

— NORDLAND
— TROMS
— FINNMARK

1. Vennesund
📍 65.2160, 12.0423

By ferry dock outside the campsite.

1058

2. Brønnøysund
📍 65.4788, 12.2167

Valveien 48, Brønnøysund - Motorhome parking at 65.4711, 12.2031

1042

3. Hattfjelldal
📍 65.5958, 13.9873

Hattfjelldal center on RV73

1048

4. Lauknes
📍 65.6128, 12.3647

Steinmo motorhome camp at Lauknes

1062

5. Herøy Caravan
📍 65.9558, 12.2705

Camping in Tenna

1049

6. Sandnessjøen
📍 66.0171, 12.6405

Shell - remote control door locks from the station

1037

7. Nesna
📍 66.2018, 13.0199

Sjøvegen close to Havblikk camping

1052

8. Mo i Rana
📍 66.3046, 14.1228

Langneset on E6

1053

9. Hellåga
📍 66.3138, 13.2845

Picnic area

1054

10. Skjerstølen
📍 66.7244, 13.6997

Picnic area and tourist information in Holandsfjorden.

1051

11. Røklandsenteret
📍 66.8137, 15.4011

Shell Saltdal / Saltdal tourist center (portable toilets).

1056

12. Storvika
📍 66.9605, 13.8038

Picnic area

1045

13. Nerauran
📍 67.0849, 15.3855

Picnic area in Rognan

1055

14. Fauske
📍 67.2574, 15.3847

Motorhome parking downtown, also for solid toilet tank.

1044

15. Bodø
📍 67.2808, 14.3757

Bodø center

1039

16. Rønvik
📍 67.2931, 14.4076

Esso

1040

17 Løding
📍 67.2997, 14.7390

Esso

1041

18 Innhavet
📍 67.9634, 15.9292

Shell v / E6 in Hamarøy. -Motorhome parking just at (67.9639, 15.9260).

1047

19 Leknes
📍 68.1454, 13.6182

Esso Leknes.

1060

20 Hagskaret Rasteplass
📍 68.1579, 13.6931

Toilet and filling of water.

1061

21 Lyngvær
📍 68.2245, 14.2163

Lofoten motorhome camping.

1063

22 Svolvær
📍 68.2273, 14.5601

Svolvær motorhome parking.

1064

23 Hjertholmen
📍 68.4123, 16.0086

Hjertholmen motorhome parking

1050

24 Evenes
📍 68.4961, 16.7001

Circle K

1043

25 Melbu
📍 68.5013, 14.8130

At Rema1000 (emptying solid tank)

1046

26 Kjerringnes
📍 68.6675, 15.4763

At the Esso station.

1057

27 Myre
📍 68.9150, 15.0983

Esso in Myre

1065

28 Andenes
📍 69.3035, 16.0648

Camping, free service

1038

29 Evenskjer
📍 68.5836, 16.5619

Skjærranveien - at XL Bygg.

1034

30 Sjøvegan
📍 68.8734, 17.8395

Parking for motorhomes just below Salangen Sports hall at Sjøvegan Center

1032

31 Andslimoen
📍 69.0946, 18.5956

Andslimoen

1031

32 Krogstadtunet Museum
📍 69.1203, 18.2168

Possibility of accommodation and power connection

1035

(33) Finnsnes
📍 69.2270, 17.9780

Meierigata by the sea

1030

(34) Senjatrollet
📍 69.4108, 17.2624

Landmark and parking for motorhomes

1027

(35) Tromsø
📍 69.6425, 18.9453

By Hålogaland theater

1036

(36) Skjervøy
📍 70.0291, 20.9791

Industriveien 11, filling of water, open all year round

1033

(37) Karasjok camping AS
📍 69.4689, 25.4890

Karasjok camping AS

1013

(38) Kirkenes
📍 69.7276, 30.0726

At the end of E6 at the parking lot for the steamship (hurigrutekaia). Closed for the winter..

1016

(39) Talvik
📍 70.0413, 22.9522

Shell

1009

(40) Lakselv
📍 70.0514, 24.9641

ESSO

1015

(41) Kjærringdalen
📍 70.0568, 22.4523

Picnic area

1008

(42) Tana
📍 70.2016, 28.1922

Located on the left side of the RV98 by Tana bridge when you arrive from Lakselv / Ifjord. Bad signs. You can free camping just off of 70.2022, 28.1919

1017

(43) Skaidi
📍 70.4320, 24.5053

Circle K Skaidi

1014

(44) Storvannet Camping
📍 70.6591, 23.7126

Storvannet Camping

1011

(45) Berlevåg camping & Appartement AS
📍 70.8570, 29.0988

Berlevåg camping & Appartement AS

1010

(46) Circle K Havøysund
📍 70.9951, 24.6731

Circle K Havøysund

1012

213 •

Notes

CPSIA information can be obtained
at www.ICGtesting.com
Printed in the USA
BVHW021213070819
555308BV00016B/1209/P